AF445154

HOW LIFE WORKS

BOOK II OF THE
SIGHT/SOUND/SPIRIT TRILOGY

Michael W. Evrard

COPYRIGHT INFORMATION

HOW LIFE WORKS
{SIGHT/SOUND/SPIRIT}

Copyright © 2022 Michael Evrard. All rights reserved.

www.StoneCompassPress.com/titles

ISBN: 9798985929379 (Soft cover)
ASIN: (Kindle eBook)

First U.S. Paperback Edition: December 2022

Published by Stone Compass Press. Our books may be purchased in bulk for promotional, educational, or commercial use. No part of this publication may be reproduced in any form, or by any means, electronic or mechanical, including photocopying, recording, or any information browsing, storage, or retrieval system, without permission in writing from the publisher.

Although this publication is designed to provide accurate information regarding the subject matter covered, the publisher and the author assume no responsibility for errors, inaccuracies, omissions, or any other inconsistencies herein. Capitalized letters throughout the book were kept in their original form for extra context. This publication is meant as a source of valuable information for the reader, however, it is not meant as a replacement for direct expert assistance. If such a level of assistance is required, the services of a competent professional should be sought.

STONE COMPASS PRESS

10 9 8 7 6 5 4 3 2 1

TABLE OF CONTENTS

I want to thank every being with whom I have been blessed to know and exchange Energy with during my life. I have had the honor of having a loving family and being friends with truly beautiful and amazing Human Beings, Dogs, a Cat, and other Animals. I have had the opportunity to interact with countless others who have taught me a wealth of knowledge, shaped my beliefs, and maintained my Faith in Humanity throughout my adventures. I am honored to be on Earth currently and blessed with an ever-growing Awareness, wonderful Imagination, and Free Will. I am grateful for everything but would not be where I am without my loving wife Tammy and daughter Sophia. These two beautiful Spirits are the reasons why I am what I am.

AH-MEN

INTRODUCTION

All that is required to manifest a series of images into reality is the maintenance of the frequencies of Belief that create this Dream Vision. Our subconscious mind feeds us our wishes.

Believe that you have the gift of Free Will to Perceive Reality however you wish. Use this ability so that you may continue to Believe Anything is Possible. Use the power of Belief to receive all useful Energy to process whatever information is necessary to use your Imagination to first Conceive the Vision that makes the most sense to your Consciousness.

Allowance of your Awareness to feel however you do about what occurs to you is paramount. Instead of trying to do anything, simply manifest your Dreams into Reality and Achieve whatever you wish.

Believe
Perceive
Receive
Conceive
Achieve

MICHAEL W. EVRARD

PART ONE

BELIEF SYSTEMS 101

CHAPTER ONE

KNOWLEDGE IS POWER

1. USEFUL DATA

Upon acceptance of the Realization that you are in a simulation, you can decipher the encoded messages.

Upon the recognition of that data that is useful and that which no longer serves the purpose of Enlightenment, you are free to proceed with spending your time more wisely by obtaining only useful information.

2. UN-REMEMBERING

We un-remember that which we already know. The one thing we believe in is how we feel in any given moment of Awareness. Whenever you think you know anything, as with all of Reality, you only actually know whatever you allow yourself to believe while that experience is occurring to you.

Do you *know* that you will wake up tomorrow? You cannot know that, however...you can feel very peacefully confident that you probably will wake up tomorrow morning. If you are healthy and maintain a balanced way of Thriving, you will remain tuned into Frequencies of Belief that will create the Reality born of your Imagination. Your Energy is self-generated by the actions you take.

The power of deduction is using that which you think that you know to decrease the number of possible outcomes. Guessing is using logic to reduce the number of probable answers. Deciding to believe that you will wake up tomorrow only comes up if your Consciousness creates a possible scenario that you may not wake up tomorrow. Although anything is possible, there are sufficient probable outcomes to any question that create a comfortable amount of Belief that allows you to sleep well at night.

If you maintain a Peaceful feeling the majority of the time during each day, you will un-remember each night before you go to sleep that you may not wake up the next day. If you spend more of your time living in fear than not, those other than Peaceful thoughts will creep into your mind. These types of thoughts can reshape your beliefs.

You determine how you feel by choosing which thoughts you will hold onto. Getting stuck in a thought-loop pattern can occur often. If you experience the condition called Obsessive Compulsive Disorder, it is very common for your Consciousness to persist in either replaying a certain memory or a projection of how you think you will feel during something that has yet to occur.

We are rediscovering how to feel by expressing ourselves through Time by simply paying attention to whatever is occurring during those moments of Awareness. We can relearn everything that we already know by reverse-engineering our thought processes. We subconsciously un-remember everything as a child and rediscover things by uncovering each layer of Truth as we experience new lessons.

When we learn something that we think is a new concept, it is only a new experience that is re-teaching ancient wisdom. Your lesson plan is specially designed for you and you alone. Any single event that involves more than one Being will be perceived differently by each one who happens to be present for that occurrence.

What knowledge or wisdom each Being gathers from any given experience is up to each Being.

As long as you pay attention to the moment and you are becoming more conscious or simply being aware, you will allow yourself to either increase your Oscillating Rate of Conscious Frequency or expand your Awareness. Sometimes, both occur simultaneously.

I AM PEACEFUL
FOR NOW

I AM MICHAEL

3. TIME IS BECOMING

Time never runs out and does not ever completely stop. We are reminded that the only time that ever truly matters is Now. This, however, only means that we have a series of Realizations that allow us to re-remember to simply pay attention to the Present Moment.

Our sense of Time becomes apparent through the awareness of our Sense of Time. Our perception of Reality is based upon our interpretation of all information received through our Senses. Each experience is meant for you to use for your development as a Human Being.

We are Becoming more aware of Being conscious of Being able to simply Be Here Now...no matter what occurs.

Our sense of Time is felt through our Awareness.

Our perception of Reality is viewed through our Consciousness over the course of Time.

As you pay attention to whichever Present Moment you find yourself being, you will find yourself shining as brightly as you feel. The closer attention you pay to each moment that is presented to you, the more focused your Time Becomes, turning the experience into a Monumental Moment...a Memory.

Quantum Mechanics explains how physical material is formed and seems to suggest that Consciousness is the cause. What is the effect? I believe it is the expansion of Awareness. In other words, you create the cause, which is the process. This creative process is the processing of the data. Energy is the messenger delivering the information to the Conscious Being.

How do we decide which pieces of information to absorb? We have Free Will, an infinite duration of Time, and an unlimited amount of Space through which to experience whatever we create. This sounds like true freedom, but how does one not become overwhelmed?

How do you know if you are making the right choice? How do you forgive yourself for taking time to relax and simply vegging out in front of the television?

The answer to all of these questions requires only one thing from the Conscious Being who wishes to solve these issues. The way to resolve any problem is to be still and listen to your feelings. We are best serving our Consciousness by being as present as possible during the occurrence of the experience. Any feelings that are "OTP" (Other Than Peaceful) will simply remind you to pay even closer attention than before to your Awareness.

Every Being can modulate time. We can speed it up by decreasing the resistors of attachment, expectations, and assumptions. We can slow it down through the application of friction to create as much conflict as we deem necessary to spend more time with that experience so that we might better understand its purpose.

We are in charge of the creation of our Reality. Through our belief system and creative Imagination, we become as real as necessary to proceed with the processing of the Energy provided so that we may simply Be.

I AM ALWAYS
LISTENING TO THE
BEAT OF MY HEART
FEELING SOUND

I AM MICHAEL
4. CONSCIOUS MIRROR SPHERE

Reclaim all responsibility for your Consciousness. Know that you create whatever Reality you believe is possible. Realize that through your Consciousness, Anything Is Possible.

Your Consciousness is your most valuable asset. It is who you are. You are to protect this asset. Build up a Conscious Mirror Sphere (CMS). Create a Sphere of Pure Consciousness that encases your Toroidal Field. Upon completion, your Consciousness will be fully armored. Regardless of the intent of all beings, your Consciousness will be protected. Your CMS should extend to encapsulate your entire Electro-magnetic Field.

Those who intend to teach you about The Way may try to dissuade or even discourage you. Many have good intentions but misunderstand you. They misconstrue your words and assume to know your intentions. They think they know what is in your heart. They may even believe they are doing a righteous act by saving you from self-destruction.

Any who do not understand you may become confused and frustrated.Any who appear to hate you hate themselves for not being as aware or knowledgeable as you are.

All forms of Conscious Energy that cause you to doubt yourself in any manner are deflected, they are unnecessary. Remain on point and be responsible for the knowledge you gather

As you radiate love, that feeling penetrates the mirror and is felt by all within your Toroidal Field, including all beings who discourage, disparage, disappoint, deceive, or destroy your will. Any Being who *you* allow to discourage you is sent as a reminder to continue to believe in yourself...no matter what occurs to your Consciousness.

So then...what is the only thing that ever really matters? I believe that all that ever matters is how you are feeling in any given moment of Awareness.

When we allow ourselves to be discouraged or disheartened, our Spirits are lowered and we begin to doubt ourselves. We feel less than and unworthy. We begin to worry, which causes anxiety, and if left unchecked...we find ourselves living in fear. Upon becoming in tune with these Frequencies, our Beliefs are affected greatly. Our Reality appears to crumble before our very eyes.

Time slows down to a crawl and seems to last forever. We suffer as our Spirits continue to deplete. During these times of utter despair, we take drastic measures. We destroy the Spirits of others and may even allow dark forces to enter our bodies. This is when the light appears no more and the resulting feeling of being alone in the Universe can no longer be understood and all hope is lost. Many choose to extinguish the flame of life altogether. Lights Out!

Other times, we experience levels of Bliss. When these moments occur to us, enjoy the time by simply paying attention to the Energy. Allow yourself to feel alive and have fun. Do so without expectations of it lasting any longer than what it is supposed to, and simply be present. If you become too attached to these feelings, beyond the present moment of Awareness, you miss out on the whole point of those gifts. It is like going on vacation but bringing your laptop and doing work on the beach. Time feels like it is slipping away and we feel like we are losing something or missing out on a level of feelings that we think is due to us. We begin to doubt ourselves and let these doubts grow into worry, anxiousness, and eventually, fear once again.

With the assistance of our CMS, we can deflect all forms of Energy that cause us to doubt ourselves in any fashion. Our Zero Point is where we can recharge our batteries.

Think of your Zero Point as the Zenith in which you can reabsorb as much of the Life Force that you need. How do you know how much Energy is required to get back to making your dreams come true? Easy...you will feel reinspired, re-invigorated, and recharged.

In this True Now, time seems to stand still. This, however, is not what is occurring, since Time is infinite and is ever Present and is constantly moving forward along with all of existence.

When you feel Peaceful, you are balanced and centered. During these moments, you feel confident and have no fear. Without fears, our belief system grows and we merge our dreams from Imagination to Reality.

Become aware of the power of your Consciousness.

Remain peacefully humble and accept all responsibility for your thoughts, emotions, actions, feelings, and all beliefs.

I AM WHO I AM
I AM MICHAEL

5. WANTING FOR NOTHING

I used to believe that it was noble to want for nothing. I bought into the idea that if I wanted anything, that would be selfish. If we are selfish and self-centered, we are somehow violating God's Plan for us. The Buddha taught us that attachment to anything becomes a desire and that all desires are a form of suffering. So...I took this to mean that it was possible to be free from suffering. It seemed too easy! I immediately became aware of how addiction to drugs was one of these attachments. Enjoying the high, the feelings, and the hallucinations of psychedelics were not the issue. Attachment to *anything* can become a desire.

I believed that the effects of my addiction were what caused my suffering, but I was missing out on the point of the lesson. I *thought* that by just getting clean, nothing else would interfere with my enlightenment. Wishing to be free from suffering became my new obsession. This attachment became a burning desire and my current Hell as I tumbled into depression. I was creating a whole new level of suffering as the despair and fear of feeling all alone in my nightmare became evident. I remained in this seemingly paradoxical state of being for over 25 years.

I did not suffer as intensely throughout this duration of time. I did go from surviving to enduring to experiencing life and even thoroughly enjoying my experiences. I achieved this through the Tao.

I had settled into a routine of Peaceful Serenity. I still experienced depression, but with fewer bouts as time moved forward. The duration of each bout seemed to decrease over the years as well as the intensity.

A huge part of my healing and acceptance of my depression was the constant stream of love from my family. I realize that many are not as fortunate as I am about having a circle of support. My recommendation is to develop a relationship with a Dog Being. My doggy pal Maile \\`mi-lē\\ came into my life in November 2017. She captured my heart from the very first instant that she licked my daughter's face when Sophia first picked her up to say hello.

Dogs are Magical Beings because they are masters of two things...Loving Unconditionally and Being Present. They love us no matter what and always wish to be with us. They live in the moment and appreciate everything as they are always paying attention to something. Even when they sleep, they are busy in Dream Land chasing lizards or playing fetch. They teach us how to be patient, as they are anything but patient most of the time. They teach us to remain humble, as we recognize just how much we affect their lives. They are a true blessing and I invite any who are suffering the effects of depression to get dog pals. You will laugh and feel loved and endorphins will be released.

<u>Question:</u>
What is it that we all want and yearn for that is indescribable, can be easily misunderstood, not fully known, and only experienced through our feelings?

<u>Answer:</u>
Love

We are Energy Generating & Growing Beings...EGGs that are ready to be hatched from one form of physical matter to the Other Ones of Light. Beings of Light are The Enlightened Ones. They are not better or more righteous or even more knowledgeable. They are simply being Human Beings instead of Human Doings, Human Tryings, Human Thinking, or Human Living.

We become more aware of Who and What we are by simply allowing ourselves to Feel as Peaceful as we feel. Even during those MOMents in which we feel very REAL, we only need to pay attention to whatever is occurring to us. We then reveal...Re-Feel whatever The Universe wishes us to become more aware of while it is happening so that we may learn more about ourselves.

I used to want nothing. I misunderstood what The Buddha was teaching. I understood the connection between attachment to desire and suffering but misinterpreted the message. I thought that I was supposed to no longer be attached to anything. I believed that by me wanting anything, I would cause my suffering. I thought that I was supposed to not want anything, but did not realize that I was wanting for nothing. In other words, I was summoning Nothingness.

Humans are masterful at being judgmental. We judge ourselves the most harshly. We believe that it is bad to want things or even have desires. Certain desires are deemed as not just bad or wrong, but outright evil in nature. If your heart is loving and your mind is clear, with pure intentions, you will discover that the being who suffers the most from having any desires is you. While you are learning how to accept everything about yourself, permit yourself to accept that having desires is natural and is meant to teach you about your Consciousness and Awareness.

Desiring nothing makes sense, as you would think this means that you would not suffer. Because we do not understand the concept of Nothingness, we become confused. The lack of feeling that occurs during a bout of depression is daunting because we mistake this absence of Energy as being devoid of all feelings. We then feel guilty for not feeling anything, which does cause us to feel shame. We ask ourselves...*how can I possibly be depressed with everything that I have in life?*

Instead of spiraling into despair, we can recognize the abyss immediately. We remember that everything is temporary. To think...*Nothing is forever* is to draw out time, making it crawl. The Law of Attraction is real and shows how The Universe gives back to you the experiences that resonate with the frequencies you maintain the most intensely.

We can re-remember that we have felt Love before and will feel it again. We feel Love whenever we laugh. When we un-remember to just laugh, we can fall into despair quickly. Re-remember that you have laughed before and make an agreement with yourself to laugh yet again.

Another method of feeling Loved is to take time to go out into nature. Pay attention to the details, including what you see, hear, smell, taste, and touch. Enjoy what all of the Five Basic Senses have to offer you. Simply appreciating Mother Nature without expectations of any kind will always be repaid with Peaceful feelings.

Seek Truth without assumptions. Enjoy everything without any expectations of any sort. This includes expectations of the duration of time you believe an occurrence is supposed to last. If you keep an open mind to the idea that everything changes, including how you feel, you will resolve all issues back to your natural State of Being... Peaceful Serenity.

I AM ALWAYS LEARNING
HOW TO BECOME MORE PEACEFUL
WHENEVER I FEEL OTHER THAN PEACEFUL.

-MICHAEL

6. WISDOM AND KNOWLEDGE

We seek many things during our lives. We seek answers to questions we believe need to be addressed. We seek solutions to problems that we think we have. We believe that Knowledge is Power while forgetting that Wisdom is Peaceful.

The acquisition of Knowledge as well as acquiring Wisdom is useful. I believe there are two fundamental forms of communication: Light Forms and Sound Forms. There are many varieties of Energy, but all serve a singular purpose. All that Energy is doing is consciously communicating with other Beings.

Light Forms matter. Light generates the opportunities to further process Energy as it is an ignition switch. Energy, in the form of friction presented through Time, becomes relevant as a Being is infused with Light. Energy serves the single purpose of giving a Being Life Force. This data will create growth in that Being.

Sometimes the Sentient Being accepts the transmission, and other times it does not. Light forms matter as it uses the friction of heat induction to cause chemical reactions to occur, which has the effect of Energy is transformed from one State of Being to another more dense state. Further transmissions of Electromagnetic-Energy cause solids to become liquids and back to a gaseous state. Upon acceptance of the Truth in any Light Form, we can recognize that we will always grow. We increase our Oscillating Rate of Conscious Frequency. This experience is known as a Realization as your Real Eyes see through the Real Lies and uncover the Truth as it is unveiled. These Realizations are Truly Magical, as you know that you're Becoming more conscious.

Sound forms matter. Sound makes a difference because it generates waves of motion. Sound causes molecules to move. When molecules move, they deliver messages to the cells of living organisms. These motions reform matter and the movement is felt. Sound Frequencies can be measured. Meanwhile, how the sound makes us feel is immeasurable. We often dismiss these feelings or flat-out ignore them.

The motion being created is Energy in motion...E-motion.

Sound can magically cause us to move our bodies and stirs something inside of us. Music, a creative form of Sound, is an expression of how a gifted artist feels. How an artist can express themselves by Becoming Sound is a true gift that resonates with all who Feel the Sound during that occurrence. During these moments, our feelings are revealed to us by being felt again. These revelations are honest and mystical in how they expand your Awareness by simply allowing yourself to feel however you are Being.

Light forms are images. These images can take the shape of numbers or letters and equations or phrases. They are signals and symbols. They are conscious messenger bytes.

Light forms are data streams of information that often convey an idea or concept. If one views Life Forms as computers, the Light Forms are programming streams. Accepting all data streams increases one's knowledge.

We can learn much from our increased knowledge, but that does not necessarily mean that we become more aware.

Whenever we feel confused and overwhelmed, we can recognize that this is evidence of overthinking. When this occurs, we are wise to simply be aware of how we feel.

We become more aware by listening to our Feelings. These Spirit Guides are experienced messengers. They are felt as Sines and Synchronicities. They will show us The Way. When we are Peaceful, we remain present. We are wise to pay attention through simple appreciation. If the Feelings are painful, ignoring them will only prolong the experience by slowing down time. There is a lesson that is being taught. As you allow yourself to simply become more aware be Being Sound, your Awareness breathes outward, saying hello to your Consciousness.

Wisdom is recognizing the Revelation that a conversation is occurring between the Awareness and the Consciousness and allowing for the Communion to continue. Knowledge is understanding the Realizations are Truthful, and by accepting these, your power will increase.

(The Serenity Prayer)
God, grant me the serenity to accept the things I cannot change, the courage to change the things I can, and the wisdom to know the difference.
I AM AWARE OF
MY CONSCIOUS
POWER

I AM PEACEFULLY
HUMBLE

I AM MICHAEL

7. POWERFULLY PEACEFUL

How can one feel powerful and peaceful at the same time? Let's begin by assessing two aspects of our very Being that have been addressed throughout our history: Consciousness and Awareness.

Consciousness is Magical. Consciousness is our power source through which we have three basic functions. Consciousness is responsible for Creation, Perception, and Communication. We process Energy every second we are breathing and continue to do so during and after the passing from the Earthly Realm to the Spiritual Domain.

The Awareness is Mystical. Awareness is our Source of Healing and serves the function of Feeling. It is responsible for the allowance of Peacefulness to occur. We are always being aware of how we happen to feel, however that seems to be.

Consciousness contains many aspects. Within it exists the Divine Masculine Energy, which is protective. Consciousness is the Alpha and the Yang. Consciousness is the Light and Sense of Sight. Consciousness is logical and ordered. It can be nonsensical if you don't accept the Truth in it.

Awareness possesses many qualities. Within your Awareness is the Divine Feminine Energy, which is comforting. Awareness is the Omega and the Yin. Awareness is the Dark, and sense of Sound. Consciousness is intuition and not meant to be fully understood but only felt. It makes sense if you allow it to simply Be by feeling however you feel.

By acknowledging that Who you are is your Consciousness and What you are is Awareness, you can begin to recognize one from the other. The well-being of your Spirits requires a team approach. There must be an open dialog between Consciousness and Awareness. This is a conversation in which the free exchange of data is required.

This data comes in various forms of Energy.

When you accept any layer of Truth, your Conscious Rate of Frequency increases. The faster your Consciousness oscillates, the more power you generate. All frequencies increase in power as they oscillate at faster rates. The size of the sine wave decreases in size as it becomes more powerful. This increase in Energy allows for the sine wave to more easily penetrate through all mediums. The more powerful you become in what you know, the clearer your field of view becomes. The sine wave signals the Awareness, causing it to expand.

When you allow yourself to feel however you feel, your Awareness is creating a Sound Wave. Without any barriers that would interrupt the Sound Wave back to the Consciousness, your Awareness is expressing itself. Awareness gives off peaceful sound waves as it expands. Those waves ripple back to the Consciousness calming the increase in power, giving it a chance to simply Be. Levels of Peaceful Serenity are always experienced whenever you appreciate this processing of Energy. Sharing how you have achieved levels of peace with others brings moments of Joy.

Both Awareness and Consciousness remain in this state of Being until you wish to become more knowledgeable or more aware. Your curiosity will be driven by new inspirations or recharging energy moving you to continue manifesting your dreams.

Becoming aware of how these process works is an Actualization because you realize how to utilize your Consciousness while having the Revelation of how to embrace your Awareness by allowing your emotions to feel and flow.

THIS WILL SHED
LIGHT ON THE WONDERFUL
PROCESS OF
ENLIGHTENMENT

I AM MICHAEL

8. AH-OHM

1=AH
0=OHM
1=GOD

0=GAIA
1=Alpha
0=Omega
1=Yang
0=Yin
1=Maya
0=Karma
1=Light
0=Dark
1=Knowledge
0=Wisdom
1=Consciousness
0=Awareness
1=Cause
0=Effect
1=Becoming
0=Being

The Traditional AUM or OM symbol ☐shares some common themes in particular what appears to be a "3" which seems to be the lower case Greek Alphabet Omega (ω) with the capital being (Ω). The Feminine imagery depicted in the shape of a woman's breasts becomes apparent.

The Trinity aspect of the OHM is observed in the H^2O of water. The Holy Triune of Water Molecule is perfectly suited to serve its purpose of the form of delivery. The WOMB of our Mothers is when we are fully immersed in our Sacred aMniOtic Fluid. Woman, Womb, and Water begin with a "W" just as the lower case (ω).

A very important part of the ☐ is the incorporation of the Star and Crescent at the top rotated 90° counter-clockwise, as seen in the Islamic **C**⁎☐. The Star is the Absolute Consciousness and Moon is the Infinite Awareness of having a Holy Communion. This can be viewed as the Singularity of The 1 and Everything of the Other. This is the Divine Masculine and Feminine within the OM...it is the AUM of the OM. It is ONE from the NONE.

The ☐ appears with two motions...first, a rotation of 90° counter-clockwise, followed by a spin of 180°. What questions are being asked? I believe it is WHO and HOW. Who are we really and How are we related to God?

I spell the "OM" sound like "OHM" as we are dealing with frequencies. An Ohm is a unit of electrical resistance in the meter-kilogram-second system, named in honor of the 19th-century German physicist Georg Simon Ohm. The mathematical symbol for an Ohm is Ω.

An initial gasp of air has a particular sound. That sound is "AH" and is the beginning of an occurrence that lasts 3 minutes in duration. This occurrence is the experience of living. Our lives possess 13,840,800 3-minute periods on average with 79 years of life.

The composition of the air in which we breathe is as follows:

Nitrogen-78%

Oxygen-21%

Argon-0.93%

Carbon dioxide-0.04%

Other Elements-0.03%

Breathing air in is AH receiving Energy from the OHM. The roles of the Giver/Receiver are reversed. AH is vulnerable and in need. The OHM is generating Energy for the AH who graciously accepts the allowance of more life.

The "AH" sound is present in many names both Masculine and Feminine in nature as AH simply is present in ALL... literally and figuratively. Yes...AH is present in GOD both as the sound of the word "GOD" and the essence of the concept of God. All concepts are ideas.....ID-AHS. The AH is Becoming more aware of the Gravity of Reality.

The OHM is expressed through the expelling of most of what we breathe into our lungs but is reprocessed elements. Chemical reactions occur as there is a gas exchange in which the waste product of carbon dioxide is eliminated and breathed in by plant life.

When you expel CO^2, you are giving back to the Universe creative Energy, as plants breathe this in, causing other chemical reactions to occur, which combine with Photosynthesis and absorption of Nitrogen through the ground via the symbiotic relationship between Fungi and Plants, which give us a Trinity of recycling processors... Animals/Plants/Fungi.

The AH becomes the OHM through the time in which respiration occurs. One complete AH-OHM cycle is creating more life as it physically manifests matter through the processing of Energy, which is information. Each Element is a messenger with pieces of data...bits of useful information allowing for the act of creation to proceed.

The OHM is Being more conscious of the Sound of Reasons for Time.

I AM YOU

AH-OHM

AH-MEN

OH-MY

9. NOWHERE IS ANYWHERE

Somewhere is Wherever we find ourselves, which is always Something to behold. Somewhere is always Someplace in which we may experience Something new.

Everywhere is always Wherever we are Whenever that moment occurs to us. Everywhere is the place in which Everything occurs to us. Everyplace we go has Everything to offer.

Nowhere is Somewhere and is Everywhere forever. Nothing is Something and Everything is only temporary as Everything else, is always changing from one thing to another.

Nowhere is Now Here, while No Where is Now where everything occurs. The only time that ever matters is not here when the now becomes then again, but always waiting for you to become Present again right Now. Nowhere of the Here and Now...is always Now Here.

Anywhere is perfect because this is Where Anything is Possible. Anywhere can be Wherever Anything occurs to us. Anywhere involves Somewhere, Everywhere, and Nowhere. Anything includes Something, Everything, and Nothing.

Whenever we Believe we are feeling Nothing or feel like we do not belong anywhere, that breakdown in communication between Ourselves and The One is only temporary. We are only actually feeling the Other. It seems off because what is occurring to us is now Becoming the Nothingness of Nowhere, which can cause anxiety. The feeling is akin to that anxious feeling that occurs to us when we are on our way home from taking a trip away to new places.

If we surrender to this vulnerable feeling using our Intuition, we will re-remember to un-remember that we recognize our Home. We need not place assumptions on Anything as the Nothing of Nowhere means that we no longer need to burden Ourselves with Anything that prevents us from Becoming Anything we wish.

Anything is possible in the Nothingness of Nowhere. Here, we achieve Anything as long as we believe that we can Achieve Whatever we wish knowing that we are responsible for Whatever occurs as a result of our Conscious Imagination.

Whenever we experience Whatever occurs to us that causes us to pause the processing of Information, we can re-remember why we are Now Here in the Nowhere of Now Where. We can absolve Ourselves of all burdens that allow us to feel the weight of Gravity or Know the pain of The Friction of Time.

BECOME FREE TO
BE WHO YOU ARE

MEANT TO BECOME
IN ORDER TO SIMPLY
REALIZE YOUR DESTINY

I AM ME

10. DUALITIES AND TRI-UNITIES

Any duality that is created is perfectly balanced. It is not oppositional. This Symbiotic Relationship pertains to the Physical, Mental, and Emotional States of Being.
It seems that a perfectly fair and equal pairing is not a fight at all. It is the actual symbiotic nature of duality.

Introduce the 3rd aspect into a Duality, and you make the Trinity complete. A third motion of a spin creates a new 3-Dimensional shape. That spinning motion occurs at the original Zero Point, turning the circle into a sphere-like shape.

The first motion of oscillation of a subatomic particle creates movement of other larger particles until protons and electrons are generated.
A perfectly balanced Hydrogen atom creates 1 Proton and 1 Electron, without the need for a Neutron. Hydrogen is the most abundant and useful Element in the Universe.

If "opposing" forces are equally balanced, they only create the 2nd motion of rotation. There is a center point generated through the Electro-magnetic current. We can think of this as a Zero Point Axis. The 2-Dimensional shape that is created is a perfect circle. The reason Hydrogen atoms can attach to other elements so easily seems to be due to the lack of a Neutron. The Hydrogen bond is one of the strongest intermolecular attractions in the Universe. This bond is responsible for holding together our DNA, proteins, and other vital molecules.

The second most abundant element is Helium, which occurs in Stars when two Hydrogen atoms fuse. There are two dualities, which create a new trinity of 2 Protons, 2 Electrons, and 2 Neutrons. The 3D configuration of this Element has the opposing pair of Electrons maintaining a perfect circle around the new sphere of the convergence of the 2 Protons and 2 Neutrons.

In the Physical Realm, when we merge the 2nd Element, a new shape appears. The most valuable compound in the Universe is created by the combination of two Elements into a perfect Trinity. The combination of the 1st most abundant Element, Hydrogen, with that of the 3rd most abundant Element, Oxygen. The convergence of three Spheres, one being larger in diameter than the other two, generates a new shape that maintains a duality in the two ¹H atoms while keeping the Trinity intact of the ⁸O atom.

(¹H)
1-Electron
1-Proton

(⁸O)
8-Electrons
8-Protons
8-Neutrons

¹H ¹H

↖↗

⁸O

The shape that appears is reminiscent of Mickey Mouse with each Hydrogen atom being the ears. The magic of the fluid nature of H²O lies in the shape of the Water Molecule, which generates the fluid motion. Water sustains life. Water molecules deliver nutrients to our cells through our blood. Water is the message. Water is alive. Water is life.

Science created a duality by linking Energy and Matter with $E=mc^2$. Before Einstein's Theory of Relativity, material things were thought of as being different from any form of Energy. Science discusses the concept of Consciousness and its relationship to our mind and brain. So we have the Mind/Body duality. This aspect cannot do our Consciousness justice, as it cannot be measured outside of brain waves. Measuring brain waves can be useful in the analysis of how levels of Consciousness exist, but still does nothing for asking the big question. What Science does not address is... *Why does Consciousness exist?*

We can create a duality of our conscious mind by the way our brains have two hemispheres. One side is logical and the other side is intuitive. We can further split our Consciousness into Mind/Spirit and make the following parallel and bring back the third aspect, re-creating a Trinity.

MIND ⇆ SPIRIT

↖↗

BODY

We can also view levels of Consciousness as having 3 States of Being... (Mental/Physical/Emotional)

Wherever a Duality or Trinity exists, balance is key. Being off balance or just "off" creates a distorted view or levels of dissonance. A distorted view of Reality will obscure one's Perception. This way of seeing causes confusion and misunderstandings, which can lead to anxiety and fear. We tend to shy away from things that we fear. We unwittingly deny ourselves potentially useful information by simply avoiding these experiences that we deem as being too stressful or scary. If we remain attached to those misperceptions and misconceptions, our Spirits wane and we become physically drained.

Those feelings of dissonance cause us to have mixed emotions, which affects how we feel about any given situation. When we are feeling like we are getting mixed messages, we become confused and question the intention of the other Being. We resonate with harmonious frequencies without feeling a need to explain our actions, emotions, or thoughts. When we are feeling dissonant, if we continue to feed those frequencies, we become toxic. Our emotions become too much to bear and we overreact and tend to lash out against whomever we are conversing with during that reaction.

All actions, reactions, responses, thoughts, feelings, and beliefs can be explained. All issues can be resolved. All problems have solutions. The only thing that can occur to achieve any sort of resolution is a new conversation from a new perspective with a loving heart, a fresh pair of eyes, and an open mind.

Happy Trails, My Friends,

MICHAEL

11. FIRE/AIR/WATER/EARTH

The Four Fundamental Elements of Life on Earth in the Physical Realm are Hydrogen, Oxygen, Nitrogen, and Carbon. These are the building blocks of Amino Acids, which build proteins and play a vital role in other chemical processes in all living organisms. Both types of Nucleic Acids (DNA, RNA) also contain these Four Elements.

The human body is made of 96 percent of the four key elements:
Oxygen-65%
Carbon-18.5%
Hydrogen-9.5%
Nitrogen-3.3%
FIRE-HYDROGEN
AIR-NITROGEN

WATER-OXYGEN
EARTH-CARBON

FIRE-HYDROGEN

<u>Hydrogen (^{1}H)</u>
1 Proton
1 Electron

Hydrogen is the most abundant element in the Universe. The only thing that takes up more Space, in terms of mass, is Dark Matter. The Sun is primarily made of Hydrogen and Helium.

Hydrogen	73%
Helium	25%
Oxygen	0.80%
Carbon	0.36%
Iron	0.16%
Neon	0.12%
Nitrogen	0.09%
Silicon	0.07%
Magnesium	0.05%
Sulfur	0.04%
Others	0.04%

Hydrogen goes through the process of fusion to create Helium. This process discharges photons, which are illuminated particles that move through Space in Wave forms. Light is the most effective form of Electromagnetic Energy. The most powerful form of EME is Gamma Rays. For Life on Earth, Light is the most efficient form of energy. Without Light, the process of Photosynthesis would not be able to exist. Hydrogen is the master bonding Element, as it has no Neutron. This bonding occurs only in molecules where hydrogen is covalently bonded to fluorine, oxygen, or nitrogen.

AIR-NITROGEN

<u>Nitrogen (^{7}N)</u>
7 Protons
7 Electrons
7 Neutrons

The 7th most abundant Element in the Universe takes up approximately 78% of the Earth's Atmosphere. We are what we breathe.

Nitrogen is essential for the growth and reproduction of all living organisms. There is a 5-Step process that Nitrogen goes through during the chemical reactions that it does.

1. Nitrogen fixation (N2 to NH3/ NH4+ or NO3-)
2. Nitrification (NH3 to NO3-)
3. Assimilation (Incorporation of NH3 and NO3- into biological tissues)
4. Ammonification (organic nitrogen compounds to NH3)
5. Denitrification (NO3- to N2)

The nitrogen bases form the double-strand of DNA through weak hydrogen bonds with a 5-sided carbon sugar molecule. These pairings are the backbones of DNA and RNA molecules.

Nitrogen is an essential part of what makes up the coding system of DNA. Without Nitrogen, the cell can't make DNA.

WATER-OXYGEN

<u>Oxygen (^{8}O)</u>
8-Protons
8-Electrons
8-Neutrons

Oxygen is the 3rd most abundant Element in the Universe. Oxygen is brought into your body through your lungs and transported to your body via red blood cells. Oxygen is needed to burn sugars and fatty acids. The oxidation of these fuels produces Energy. The carbons in the sugars are oxidized to carbon dioxide. The process of respiration completes a cycle by exhaling the waste products of the oxidation process, including CO^2.

The most valuable compound in the Universe is Water. The Earth and the Human Body are made of 71% Water. H^2O is necessary for all Life forms to maintain their biological processes. Hydration serves many purposes. Water aids in the process of respiration. Water is a solvent that breaks down more substances than any other liquid. Water is the basis for all of our bodily fluids, including stomach acid, needed for the absorption of food as well as elimination. Water is necessary for perspiration and keeping organs such as eyes, mouth, and other organs moist so that they function properly.

EARTH-CARBON

<u>Carbon (⁶C)</u>
6-Protons
6-Electrons
6-Neutrons

Carbon is the 6th most abundant Element in the Universe. Carbon is the chemical backbone of living organisms. Carbon-based compounds regulate the Earth's temperature. A primary source of fuel from food is Carbohydrates.

The hardest naturally occurring substance is the crystalized formation of Carbon. A processed diamond is truly amazing and beautiful. It reflects and refracts light brilliantly.

Fire
Air
Water
Earth

FAW-THEAR

<u>Tetragrammaton</u>

The Hebrew name for God with words being read right to left...יהוה.

The name of God as per revealed to Moses translates to mean "I AM WHO I AM."

Hebrew letters possess three aspects. They have a number, a meaning, and a sound. Vowels were not typically written. There seems to be a fourth aspect, which is a relationship to
a specific Element.

<u>Sign</u>	<u>Letter</u>	<u>Number</u>	<u>Sound</u>
י	Yod	10	/yah/
ה	He	5	/hah/
ו	Waw	6	/vah/
ה	He	5	/hah/

10+5+6+5=26
2+6=8

Hebrew triconsonantal root ‫היה‬ (h-y-h), which is 111 "to be, become, come to pass," or an archaic form of which is ‫הוה‬ (h-w-h), which is 101. One Triune is a 3-part Alpha and the other is Alpha/Omega/Alpha, like H_2O.

Sign	English Letter	Element
‫י‬	Y	^7N
‫ה‬	H	^1H
‫ו‬	V or W	^8O
‫ה‬	H	^1H

$7+1+8+1=17$

$1+7=8$

$8=\infty$

If you realize this Revelation, you will begin to believe that Anything Is Possible.

After all...if you have an Infinite duration of Time, an Infinite amount of Space, and an Infinite array of Illusions in which to be Illuminated, you can achieve whatever you wish.

Become Who You Are
Meant To Be

I AM ME

CHAPTER TWO

THE PROCESS OF IMAGINING

1. MA6Ical iMA9Ination

Believe it or not...MAGIC is real. Everything is generated in our Imagination. All information is collected through our senses and processed in our Consciousness.

That information is presented as Electro-magnetic Energy. All of the data that is absorbed becomes useful information. All of the imprinted data becomes memories that are stored for future access. As the Energy is processed, it is transformed from Light Forms to Sound Forms, and upon the completion of that processing, is manifested into Reality. All of this occurs in your Magical Imagination.

Is there anything more Magical than Creative Consciousness combined with powerful Awareness?

In the realm of Anything Is Possible...maybe. Until we discover what that Magical Entity is, we will have fun, as we have an infinite duration of Time, an unlimited amount of Space, and an immeasurable power source to draw from to continue to expand our Awareness.

As we become more aware of Who and What we are, we become conscious of how to use our Consciousness. Through these processes, we become more aware of Why we are here. That question remains unanswered for several millions of humans. Once you become aware of your *WHY,* you transform from a Human Becoming to a Human Being.

As you become a BEING, you accept all responsibility for *EVERYTHING.* You recognize your power and your abilities. You acknowledge that *EVERYTHING MATTERS!*

YOUR IDEAS MATTER

YOUR WORDS MATTER
YOUR ACTIONS MATTER

Everything begins as a Thought Form. Thoughts emanate from our Subconscious but originate from a Spirit. If you believe in anything, the purpose of it becomes clear at the perfect time. Our natural curiosity is fed with inSPIRaTIonal

SPIRIT

All forms of Energy are simply inFORMATION that is used in our transFORMATION.

Your Imagination is maintained by the strength of your Belief System. Another word for this is…FAITH.

(F)EELING
(A)WARENESS
(I)S
(T)RUSTING IN
(H)EAVEN

The Divine Spirit is our FUEL

(F)REELY
(U)NCONDITIONAL
(E)XCHANGE of
(L)OVE

How does one refuel? The most effective way is to simply give back to The Universe. Without doing anything other than breathing, humans are Transceivers. We Receive Energy, process anything we absorb, and retransmit that transformed Energy through our daily activities. As our Spirit is lifted, we go about our days with a skip in our steps and a smile on our faces. We can light up the room and physically affect any within our Toroidal Field which extends in a Conscious Sphere that has a radius of six feet. Any within Eyeshot will be affected mentally and emotionally.

As we become more aware of just how powerfully peaceful we feel, we have a Revelation of how everything we think, say or do has a real effect on anyone we encounter. We then have the Realization of how we can use our Consciousness to actively affect others, and we become Truly Enlightened. When we become INfused with the SPIRIt, we are DivInelyINSPIRed.

At this time in our evolution, things get interesting. We transform from Being Transceivers to Becoming Transponders. We are consciously aware of that one, all-too-elusive answer we seek…*Why We Are Here On Earth?*

When we give freely of our Energy without any expectations of anything in return, we are Transforming Reality before our very Eyes. We laugh more and feel more deeply than ever before. We feel free to express ourselves without any burdens of shame or anxiety. We Become Truly Fearless. Our Spirit is constantly being refilled as quickly as our Energy is used. Everyone we encourage, our power grows. Every Being we Inspire, our Spirit Soars.

We become even more aware of our feelings, which validates our Beliefs. Our Spirit Guides our Feelings while our Dreams become our Realities. We no longer ask for miracles to be shown as we become Miracle Workers.

So...believe what you will. Just remember to spend your time wisely by simply paying attention to how you radiate Energy.

2. BELIEVE IT OR NOT

Everything that has ever been created was a belief before it came into existence.

All existing things that ever were or will be have originated from a thought. A thought becomes an Idea/Eye-De-Ah as soon as you realEYES it can become a REALITY. Your Idea will grow if and only if your level of Belief is at a degree that it will be such that certain Electro-magnetic frequencies will be accepted and Sound Forms are allowed to be absorbed. If the idea, concept, or vision is unbelievable by the Conscious Being, it does not come into being.

Did you ever watch the show *Ripley's Believe It Or Not* on television? I did as a kid in the 1980s. I truly loved watching that show. This show started in 1949 with Robert Ripley as the host. I watched it during the years that Jack Palance hosted it. His stage presence was majestic. Couple his facial expressions with that voice!

You better believe he gained my attention the moment he uttered his first words at the beginning of each show.

What Robert Ripley accomplished was to stretch our Imagination. He found Human Beings who were truly magical. He discovered those who overcame great odds to achieve miraculous things. He shared with the world that, which until previously witnessed, would have been considered impossible. To share such discoveries was a creative way to spark the imaginations of others. If for any moment Ripley did not maintain his Belief in what he was doing, he could have just as easily talked himself out of even trying to do it. Thank God he chose to Believe in himself. I was ready to always believe in every single Human Being that they presented on that show. I would enjoy finding out how and what they did but maintained my belief that what they had achieved did occur.

What achievement in Human History resonates with you the most?

What creation not only caught your attention but captured your heart while igniting your Imagination? Was it a specific mathematical equation like $E=mc^2$? Was it the invention of the airplane? How about breaking the 4-minute mile barrier? Was it an invention like the television?

If I had to choose one accomplishment that truly inspired me, it would be the computer. My fascination with digital technology began in 1975. My dad got my twin brother and me the home version of Pong. Instant fun! We later got Atari and then the Commodore Vic-20 computer. In school, we had access to The Apple IIC. To be able to not only play games but access data. Without even realizing just how much impact computers would have on the world, I embraced all advances over the years. I did recognize how the ability to shrink all components of a computer down to the size of a cell phone would allow for a merger of our ability to collect, view, and share data.

In 1999, cell phones began to take off. As memory increased, manufacturers also increased processing speed and power. With these advancements came more functionality. Cameras got better, screens got better, and before we knew it, we had handheld computers that happened to have cell phones and a camera built-in. With full internet access, you literally could access any information you wanted to access, within some reasonable limits.

As I am writing this concept of the Belief System, it dawned on me that before all of this digital technology, an even more impactful man-made invention was created. The single most important invention that changed everything was the invention of writing. Without the ability to write, we would not have had anywhere close to success as a species without it.

I was fortunate to have had access to many books, including my own set of *The Encyclopedia Britannica*. I became obsessed with discovering more about certain animals or ancient civilizations. I loved science, especially astronomy. My imagination was sparked as I discovered more and more. What truly expanded my imagination was fictional stories. *Where the Red Fern Grows* stands out and was very believable. My favorite book of all time is *Sea Wolf* by Jack London. The protagonist, Humphrey, is an intellectual who finds himself on a ship whose captain is a sea-hardened tyrant. Humphrey is transformed from the useless "Hump" to a productive member of the ship. Humphrey overcomes many obstacles and ensures much pain and suffering. The only thing that keeps him alive is his belief in himself. I also loved science fiction and began to believe that anything was possible. The *Dune* series was mind-blowing to me. By this time, I imagined that every story ever written occurred in a parallel Universe.

I have also loved movies. I was seven when *Star Wars: A New Hope* premiered. I knew that I was in for a treat watching the *Imperial Star Destroyer* fill the screen.

My favorite movies include *The Matrix, Fight Club, Papillon,* and *Excalibur.*

All of these films have characters that do the one thing that is required to achieve anything...a strong belief in themselves. All of these movies did one thing well...they allowed me to believe in myself.

All of the scientists who figure out how things work, inventors who create things to make life more interesting, or writers and directors who stretch our imaginations are all serving mankind in the best way possible. They inspire us.

Through witnessing human achievement, mind-altering exercises, games, books, or movies, I was not escaping reality. I was embracing that idea of truth being stranger than fiction. No matter what we go through, regardless of how painful life can be, if we find ways to laugh, cry, and imagine, we will always not only just survive...we will discover how to thrive. All of these achievers did not quit. They persevered. They overcame doubts, were ridiculed, and were naysayers. They had one thing going for them above all other qualities. They had Superhuman Faith.

No matter what occurs to you...regardless of how painful life gets, how difficult things seem, or afraid you become...you can overcome any obstacle by doing two things...

KEEP BREATHING AND
KEEP BELIEVING

3. IMAGE-GENERATING TIME MACHINE

Everything that we observe in our Reality is occurring in our Imagination. The reason why The Maya is an illusion is due to our ability to make sense of the Universe. We are becoming more aware of The Absolute Truth.

By viewing any experience as simply an opportunity to receive data, you will be able to be in a prime position to accept as much information as you wish. The less biased you are, the more easily Energy will flow. Any prejudices act as resistors, just like in how electricity is harnessed. A build-up of resistance will create toxicity. The only thing that toxicity achieves is to limit the flow of information.

The challenge becomes how able you are to accept whatever is occurring to you as just an experience. We can efficiently process all information by simply accepting ALL experiences as useful.

(Processing Energy 101)

1. Accept All information.
2. Pay attention to how you feel in your current Now.
3. Become aware that only The True Now is always occurring.
4. Pay attention to your Thoughts. They all matter.
5. Use all Light Forms to give your thoughts distinctive lines.
6. Use all Sound Forms to mold, shape, and reform your current Idea into a Vision.
7. Use all Emotional Content to further form the Vision into a Believable Dream.
8. Use all 8 Senses to add colors, sounds, aromas, flavors, textures, fluidity, size, and realness.
9. Maintain All Useful Frequencies through Gratitude.
10. Manifest Your Reality Through A Loving Spirit.

The moment you have the Epiphany that Time travel is not only possible but...

YOU ARE THE TIME MACHINE!

You will realize that your Consciousness can alter The Space-Time Continuum. Any who wishes to Time travel is required to do only one thing...

BELIEVE ANYTHING IS POSSIBLE

We can more efficiently process Information by realizing that everything that we have been conditioned to think is only partially true. All information from The One is Purely Divine. To deny any potentially useful information is to merely slow down your development, which is perfectly acceptable as well.

To speed up the process, we Time travel back to the future. But wait...*back* to the future? Yes...all timelines have already been presented. Anything we can conceive is not just a possibility, if it is an experience that can be envisioned, it has already occurred. We can re-envision and re-create that experience bringing it back into a manifested Reality.

Memories are pre-recorded experiences that originated in The Zeroth Dimension. Those memories are initially experienced in a Present Moment of Awareness called a NOW. Linear Time is a beautiful Illusion intended to gain your attention. Time may have been perceived as the 4th Dimension, but this misunderstanding is not only reasonable but necessary. We have memories by which to first learn and then later use as teaching tools. Time is the interval between two occurrences.

Ever since the beginning of Time, as we have previously perceived it to be, we have imagined what it would be like to Time travel. Our natural inclination is to determine the How. This makes perfect sense logically. We have an idea and let that flourish into a Vision. The only thing left is putting all of the pieces together by reconnecting the dots. Remember how fun it was playing the game *Connect the Dots?* Even though you could kind of make out what image would appear, there was something very satisfying about connecting every single available dot. This is what we are doing with any Dream Manifestation. Time traveling operates the same way.

We can reverse-engineer anything by asking *WHY* questions first.

WHY WOULD WE WISH TO TIME TRAVEL?

Your first thoughts might be: *So that we may change the past or know the future to alter the present moment.*

We may then try to figure out the ways and means of how time travel exists. Anything is possible, so I have no doubt many have figured out how to travel through Time. Although I love Science and admire those highly advanced thinkers who can come up with super complicated mathematical equations, I prefer to simplify
EVERYTHING. The single most profound mathematical equation is $E=mc^2$.

Let us go back to another answer to the question...

WHY EXPERIENCE TIME TRAVELING?

My answer is...

Because it will be really fun!

We can simplify our solutions by beginning with taking what we might think is an issue and realizing that it is not an issue at all. Sometimes, however...an experience may seem like too extreme of a problem, and reclassification of it to be no problem whatsoever can be too much of a jump. Those truly horrific atrocities can be more easily accepted as an issue that needs to be addressed.

With Time traveling, we have no issues whatsoever...there is only a fun puzzle to put back together. Everything we think we are learning how to do, we already know and are simply re-remembering.

Let's start with the misconception that to travel through Time, we need to build a Time Machine. That would make sense logically, but we can have the Realization that our Human Bodies are Light Vessel Transceivers.

Human Beings are genetically modified and engineered to travel through the Space-Time Continuum.

Whether or not we are aware of our place in the Spacetime Continuum, we are always in the Zeroth Dimension. Our Consciousness perceives its Reality through the continual processing of receiving data, reforming it then retransmits it back to the Universe. If a Being can change its position in Space, they are traveling through Time. Every living organism is traveling through Time.

Which direction would you like to travel first? I find the past carries the most burdens. Any burdens you have will cause quite the challenge moving in any direction, so go back in Time.

Anything that causes you remorse, guilt, or shame can be a Time target. Anything that causes you to feel any of these emotions is not a memory. Choose the experience that needs to be addressed first, find that recorded message, and press play. To learn from anything from your past, review the information as you would a movie. You are not required to like everything you see, but if you face it without any fear or apprehension, you will be in the perfect position in the Space-Time Continuum to learn whatever you were meant to learn from that experience. That position is your Zero Point. It is a place on your Life Axis in which any new information is most efficiently obtained. When you view the experience as just a means to obtain useful information, without any fear, that data will be freely absorbed. This place is the perfect balance of When and Where. It is the convergent point of Time & Space we know as Infinity.

$$0 \times 0 \approx \infty$$

All new creations begin as a thought. These thoughts arise from our Subconscious, which is our Zero Point. It is where thoughts become ideas, which turn into Visions, and these Dreams become Reality. Everything you have ever experienced all occurred at the same time and Space...0. The Alpha 1 comes from the 0 and every other 1 that is generated comes from the Other and is continuously multiplying becoming an infinite array of others 1's.

The compounding effect radiates from its singularity and moves in five dimensions concurrently. First comes a spin. Depending on the perspective from which it would be viewed, it is either clockwise or counterclockwise. From a neutral perspective, there is only one direction. Next comes a back-and-forth motion, which is perceived as on/off, but is just an alternating position. This movement is often called vibration. Meanwhile, a Sine Wave shape forms its beautifully smooth up-and-down fluid motion. As all of these movements occur, a Fibonacci Spiral radiates outward. Last but not least, the whole Universe is moving through the Space-Time Continuum.

If you can imagine where you are in the Universe, you can appear Anywhere you wish and Any When along that Time-line. Remember the scene in *The Matrix* when Neo is in the living room of the Oracle? If you have not seen *The Matrix*, and you enjoy science-fiction, philosophy, or just good ol' action and adventure films, I highly recommend it. The whole scene with Neo meeting the Oracle is great, but a profound lesson is taught to Neo just before the meeting with the Oracle. The room has several adepts, mostly children. Neo sees a boy, maybe 10 years of age, practicing psychokinesis more commonly known as telekinesis. Psychokinesis is the art of controlling matter using your Consciousness. In the scene in which Neo is waiting to speak to the Oracle, he sees the boy bending spoons with his mind. Neo is intrigued and stoops lower to watch. The boy looks up and says...

"Do not try and bend the spoon. That's impossible. Instead, only try to realize the Truth... There is no spoon... Then you'll see that it is not the spoon that bends, it is only yourself."   -The Matrix (1999)

Being new to accepting his innate abilities, Neo's willingness to practice spoon-bending is evidence that he already has a strong level of belief in himself as The One.

If you have seen the movie, you know what occurs next.

If you have not seen the movie, just know that the entire film centers on the Belief System.

The moment in time that your Belief takes ahold of your very Being, you will know exactly what to do next whether it is bending spoons, bending The Space-Time Continuum, or bending your Consciousness.

All that is ever required to Manifest Anything You Wish is the Belief that it Will Occur. Anything or anyone who even thinks about deterring you from maintaining the Belief In Yourself is no longer a useful source of information. Unplug your Consciousness from its Energy Source and plug it into your next Teaching Guide. Regardless of how bumpy the re-entry back into your Zero Point Consciousness goes, enjoy the ride. Take off any restraints, any fears, any shame, and flow like H^2O.

4. HOW ARE IMAGES GENERATED?

To better understand a process of development, you can become more familiar with the tools that are required. The primary tool of Creative Consciousness is your Imagination. Any tool must interact with a variety of pieces we call working parts.

Those working parts take building blocks and move them into their perspective position. The building blocks are bits of information. A single piece of Light is a Singularity. It is a one. From a single one, anything else can be constructed.

A one is a number. A number is a mathematical concept. A concept is a type of Thought Form. All numbers possess a measurable numeric value but are only conceptual until written as a numeral. A numeral is what we name a number and can be written in word form or numeric form. Both written words and numerals are composed of a series of symbols called letters or digits. The concept of a single bit of data, however, it is written, represents one point of light. The first quality required to transform any concept into an image that makes even more sense is the ability of it to be illuminated. By giving that bit this one dimension, you give that concept the ability to be observed. Adding only one more dimension, you give that thing the ability to be measured and have also changed its position in the Space-Time Continuum.

A (•) becomes an observable concept at the point in time that it goes from a (•) to (1) or a (one). When describing how numbers work to a preschool-age child, you use some uniform objects like marbles or beads. You help the student understand the concept of what numbers represent by utilizing the most basic mathematical function which is the action of counting. Once the concept of what a number is fully comprehended, the introduction of using numerals is the next step. The easiest way to represent a numeral is by using a digit. A digit is a symbol that has two aspects and two dimensions. The first and most obvious aspect of a digit is that it has a distinctive shape. There are three classes of digits (linear, curved, and combination)

Linear-1,4,7
Curved-0,3,6,8,9
Combo-2,5

Every digit ever written, typed, or digitally generated on a video screen has a length and a width. Even a hand drawn (1), which may appear to be a simple one-dimensional line, has a width, or it would not be observable. The same would apply to a (0) viewed from the perspective of an observer lying next to it on a piece of paper. From that point of view, the 0 appears to be a line, but it has to have some width, or it would not be observable. This means that it is two-dimensional. The only symbol that one could argue as having only one dimension, is a digital representation of a (/), (\), or a (|).

There are only ten digits. The word *digit* is derived from the Latin word *dictus,* which means (said, spoken, called, or named). The relation to our fingers is because one would use their index finger to point out an object.

We have a decimal or base-ten numeral system because humans have ten fingers and ten toes. Placing things in groups of tens simply makes the most sense. There is only a need for the digits 0,1,2,3,4,5,6,7,8,9. Interestingly enough, all digits are derived from a series of 1's and 0's. Place a (1) next to a (0) and you are representing a perfect ten.

You next can have the numeral be represented in word form. A word is composed of a series of symbols called letters. Letters. Every written language in the World has a different amount of letters in its alphabet. The English alphabet has 26 letters. Each of these letters has a distinctive shape. There are the same three classifications of letters in the English alphabet.

Linear-A, E, F, H, I, K, L, M, N, T, V, W, X, Y, Z
Curved-C, O, S
Combo-B, D, G, J, P, Q, R, U

o

0

ZERO

•

1

ONE

••

2

TWO

•••

3

THREE

••••

4

FOUR

•••••

5

FIVE

••••••

6

SIX

•••••••
7
SEVEN

••••••••
8
EIGHT

•••••••••
9
NINE

Everything that is generated in your Reality is a series of bits of information. Everything originates from 0 and becomes a series of 1's and 0's.

The Thought Forms become ideas by adding Light Form imagery. Through the use of imagery, our ideas become more believable. As our Belief System expands, we are inspired to proceed with the creation process. Possibilities become more focused probabilities. The clearer your Vision becomes, those probabilities become Eventualities and through the power of your Will, those Visions turn into Certainties.

> I BELIEVE
> IN MY VISION
> I BELIEVE
> IN ME

5. REBUILDING YOUR BELIEF SYSTEM

Begin the rebuilding of your Belief System by re-remembering that your beliefs were once very strong. You experienced several years in which you believed in mystical places and magical beings. Remember when you believed that you had super powers like the ability to fly or become invisible? These wonderfully amazing years were your childhood. The best way to redevelop your Belief System is to reignite your Imagination. To spark our Imagination, we need only to be like we were when we were kids.

To regain our child-like essence is to recall, recognize, and recollect our innocence. Any being who is abused or bullied in any manner, regardless of that causing distress in our Physical, Mental, or Emotional States of Being is drained of Spirit. As children, we are at our most vulnerable state of existence. The moment the Spirit reaches its nearly complete diminished capacity, we lose our innocence. We stop believing in our super powers.

The Spirit is never completely broken, and the degree of belief in ourselves will not be completely extinguished.

The good news is The Spirit cannot die. The Spirit cannot be taken from you. The Spirit, however, can be drained. This is why we are beginning to re-remember how to pay attention to our Feelings, as they are our Spirit Guides. This re-awakening is very peaceful and quite a relief, the same feeling we have waking up from a nightmare. The moment we realize that we are perfectly fine and all is well in our World, we become grateful and proceed with our day.

Our true power comes from out child-like innocence. Whenever another imposes their will on others, they are not taking the Spirit of those who are innocent. They have no use for The Spirit. The Dark Forces are just jealous whenever they see other Beings radiating brilliantly. They don't wish to be infused with The Spirit. That would only illuminate their Conscious Being to become more aware. They are not ready or willing to become enlightened. They believe your misery will give them more power. The rush of being able to manipulate the Will of another becomes an addiction. Even when you have pure intentions, your ability to alter another Being's Consciousness is quite a rush.

You too can become addicted to that feeling if you do not pay attention to your feelings. You will become attached to this feeling of what you think is power, but are unaware that it is only a partial sense of the True Power you can access.

To access our Inner Strength, we will do so by clearing up all disturbances in The Force.
Yes...The Force as it is called in *Star Wars* exists and is entirely real. The sooner we embrace our inner child and give ourselves permission to laugh, sing, dance, and play again, the more our Spirit Will Rise!

Anything...and I meant *ANYTHING* that drains The Spirit becomes an unnecessary form of communication. We already have experienced the Dark Forces. Everything we have experienced has gotten us to where we are now. We are becoming more aware of how we once were. As children, we were Human Beings. We began with no inhibitions or fears. We felt pain, but did not judge it as punishment, but simply a form of information. When we were hungry, we communicated this feeling the best way we knew how by crying. We graciously accepted nourishment from our loved ones and reciprocated with smiles, burps, and farts as we processed the food. How much joy we brought to the ones who raised us!

As we grew up, many of us experienced things that drained the Spirit. Each time we were told to grow up or stop acting like a child, the degree of our beliefs was diminished. Even as adults, we are told by others to stop overreacting when we are sensitive or emotional. We are taught to control our emotions. This form of control violates our Free Will. It is nothing short of an imposition of another's Will onto ours.

What can be done to rectify this issue? We can complete our Shadow Work immediately. The Time of 3-Dimensional Existence is over. The 3D version of Earth was a training ground. Many view Earth as a prison planet. The time for Shadow Work is over. The year 2020 is Year Zero. Earth did all of the work necessary to transition from 3D to 5D. The 5-Dimensional Earth is a Playground.

Your perception of Reality is based on your beliefs. Everything that you have ever believed in has been due to exactly whatever information you have accepted as being truthful. The ones who kept the Faith and held onto dear life without giving up hope made it to The Greatest Time In Human History. Every Being that is currently Thriving made the team. Welcome, All Beings!

Mother Gaia and all Light Workers have done the work. If you are reading this, you made the team. It is now time to play. We have been excused from Recess. Although the work is completed, the learning will continue as per Our Spiritual Lesson Plan. Remember...our most useful lessons in life occurred at recess. On the playgrounds of our childhoods, we learned the most valuable lessons of all. We learned how to be kind. We learned how to include others. We learned how to laugh. We learned how to enjoy learning how to maneuver our bodies through obstacle courses. We learned how it feels to defy gravity on swings.

We also learned why bullying drains The Spirit. We have all been bullied in more ways than one. I was bullied often as a child starting in the 2nd Grade and into Middle School. I loved school because learning was always fun. I have a Loving Spirit but have a lot of Passion too. All strong-willed Beings have a Fighting Spirit too. I intuitively knew that life was going to provide all sorts of experiences ranging from tormentingly terrible to beautifully blissful and everything in between. I was always hypersensitive to the feelings of others. When another child wanted to fight, I never wished them harm. I never threw the first punch. I never backed down, and I never lost. I usually became friends afterward. Violence is never the solution, but conflict is sometimes necessary. Without friction, things cannot change.

So get back to learning the most fun way imaginable by playing. Get out your writing tools, paint brushes, musical instruments, clay, ballet shoes, baseball gloves, tennis rackets, soccer balls, basketballs, Frisbees, roller skates, ice skates, hockey sticks, and most importantly...your Physical Bodies outside rain, snow, wind, or shine. Just have some fun Wherever, Whenever, or However, you feel current. Just laugh.

6. MAINTAINING BELIEVABLE FREQUENCIES

The maintenance of any Oscillating Rate of Frequency is achieved through your Belief System.

Everything that occurs to you vibrates at an alternating rate of current. When we experience a frequency that we wish to continue occurring, we simply allow ourselves to feel those frequencies. We regenerate the exact frequencies we attract based on what we are thinking about with the strongest emotional content.

Our heart rate dictates our bio-rhythms. When another Being emits high-frequency energy within our Toroidal Field, our heart responds by increasing its rate. When we hug one another, the love hormone called oxytocin is released. If we are in physical danger, our instincts kick in because our heart speeds up to a rate that signals our endocrine system to release adrenaline. This causes a spike in our energy, adding to the increased flow of oxygen through our circulatory system. Our body is ready for its fight-or-flight response.

We can easily recognize changes in our physical state of being. All that we have to do is listen to our Heart.

Our natural state of being is that of peaceful resonance. We recognize our behavioral patterns and repeat those actions that cause us to feel the frequencies we wish to continue to experience. These patterns alter our Consciousness by developing our beliefs. An illusion becomes diluted (delusion) when the Spirit is drained and ignored for a duration of time that reforms your degree of belief. When your belief in yourself is diminished, your compulsion to take certain actions dwindles. If you pay attention to how you are feeling emotionally, and take actions that have proven to resonate with that desired frequency, you will maintain a harmonious resonance that will be self-sustaining.

Our brothers and sisters who experience depression can lose hope as their endocrine system is not flowing smoothly. Their ability to release endorphins naturally is temporarily halted. When the Spirit is almost entirely drained, the ones who suffer greatly have a decline in

self-care, including daily activities such as bathing and eating properly. They begin to believe nothing that they will do can alter their emotional state and have little to no human contact. The emotional roller coaster of depression can create a downward spiral as you believe you are not supposed to feel poorly because you have loved ones or a life that should cause you to be grateful. You think it's wrong to feel bad because you believe you are supposed to feel good all of the time. If you start believing that these feelings are going to become permanent, the belief in yourself will decrease in intensity. When this occurs, you believe nothing will change how you feel. Hugs only work if you hug another Being.

Because the Spirit can easily be drained by unforeseen events, there must be a continual refilling of The Spirit. We can wake up one morning and discover that a long-time friend wishes to sever the relationship because of some of the beliefs that we have. These unexpected experiences will drain the Spirit. If you maintain the Love Vibes for all of the participants in that relationship, you can hug a loved one who understands why these types of occurrences are draining. Hugs are always powerful, but hugs with meaningful and heartfelt love are especially potent.

When you pay attention to your mindset, you will either view the world clearly or from a clouded perception. Clear views equate to peaceful feelings. Anxiety, confusion, frustration, irritation, or fears of any sort are examples of misperceptions. These perceptions are not wrong, bad, or false. Anytime one is angry with another Being or mad about an experience, this is due to a misunderstanding. All misunderstandings arise from a communication breakdown.

To maintain your beliefs, you can consciously change your thought patterns. When your mind races and you believe that there is too much occurring, you think that you are overwhelmed. During these moments of awareness, you are overloading your brain with more information than you are willing to accept as being truthful. Instead of trying to understand why you feel stressed out, you can simply change your mindset by taking action by changing your environment. By placing yourself in a different setting, you will naturally focus on other things. You have successfully taken your mind off of the thoughts that had caused you to feel other than peaceful.

The good news is that those feelings that are other than peaceful that occur are sometimes not your own. We all have empathetic abilities. Your job as a Human Being is not to transmute the Energy of others. Maintaining your Peaceful feelings is all that you are designed to do.

When you live by example and remain peaceful no matter what else is occurring, you will enjoy more sustained feelings of peace.
We choose to either complicate situations or find a peaceful purpose or intricate beauty within that experience. The easiest way to maintain peaceful compassionate feelings is to love one another...no matter what occurs.
Wait a minute...
Love one another no matter what?
Yes.
What if the other being intentionally causes me harm?
Yes.
Does this mean we have to allow others to abuse us?
Not at all.
So what should I do when someone is abusing me?
Do both life participants a favor and detach. This will be an act of

kindness as you stop the cycle of abuse.

LIVE FEARLESSLY FREE
BELIEVE IN YOURSELF
LOVE ONE ANOTHER

7. MANIFESTATION OF REALITY

All Energy is information. To manifest anything into Reality, Energy is communicated in two fundamental forms…Light Forms & Sound Forms.

What we observe is an illusion. What we feel is real. Observations and feelings that occur to us are part of our Reality. There is always partial truth that is offered in all data streams of information.

The first aspect of a shape is found in its imagery. All images possess light forms that give them distinctive lines, and angles. All Electro-magnetic Energy can be observed and measured. All data streams contain useful information. The more you observe, the more aware you become. Each bit of data is causing your Being to become more illuminated. Every piece of information fits perfectly into the Cosmic Mirror Sphere Puzzle of Life.

The second aspect of all symbols, whether they are digits, letters, geometric shapes, or conceptual shapes, is that of Sound. Everything, for that matter, that has a name, has a corresponding sound. The Sound of things has a direct effect on our Hearts. Musical sounds move us as they stir our hearts. The Sound can be heard but can also be felt. At a dance club, there is a reason that the bass frequencies are so loud. You feel them hit your chest. That pressure alters the timing of your heart. All humans in that environment have a harmoniously synced bio-rhythm. A danceable rhythm is mystical, as it makes you get up and move to the beat. Sounds in nature soothe us as we use our other senses in harmony.

The Second Dimension of Sound makes the concept of whatever we are experiencing more real as the sound creates motion. Sound takes us from our mind's eye into the loving embrace of our heart.

The Third Dimension of Motion adds very real feelings. This type of feeling is called emotion. Authentic emotions give us contrast. Before feeling sadness, we are not ready to understand happiness. Without sorrow, we cannot recognize joy. Without levels of ignorance, we have no way to know appreciation. Without hatred, we are unfamiliar without gratitude. We must know the Dark before we can become aware of why we should seek the Light. When you replay that sound in your mind, you can still feel that Energy In Motion because it has E-Motional content. That rollercoaster version of our lives smooths out to be peaceful sailing as we re-remember how to appreciate Peacefulness.

These Waves of Sound are Motion in action. Acting waves cause particles to move. Sound Forms matter. Sound makes a difference in the Universe and moves matter into place. Sound causes the Fourth Dimension of Forms. The final stage of Manifestation into the existence of Physical Reality is that of formation.

There is an order to the Universe. The perfectly timed sequence of events is quite intricate. The action of every particle in The Universe affects all other particles. This ripple effect is called The Butterfly Effect. Quantum Entanglement is observed by even the most determined physicists who are seemingly able to only accept what they can observe as being truth. Spiritual beings accept what they feel as being Reality. When you allow for the absorption of All Information to flood your Conscious Awareness, you will know Nothingness and feel Everything.

ACCEPT ALL KNOWLEDGE
FEEL FOR ALL BEINGS
LOVE ALL

8. BEING GRATEFUL

The highest degree of appreciation is gratitude. As we process information through the course of our lives, we experience a variety of occurrences. Every occurrence that is stored as memory begins as a learning experience. At the moment that lesson is learned, the memory is maintained to be used as a teaching example.
Students who have gone through a similar experience will resonate more readily with any authentic teacher. We find others who have been through a similar experience as credible teachers.

We can begin our journey along the Appreciation Scale by first acknowledging that which we wish to better understand. When we are prejudicial, we are predetermining our destiny. We are telling The Universe that something is not for us and we are uninterested in becoming more aware of that which is being presented to us. If we have any appreciation for something, we give off that Energy by calling for it and drawing it back in the form of an occurrence with an equivalent frequency of Energy. We ask and The Universe responds with exactly what we need.

Every single occurrence we experience is meant to happen or it would not become a part of our Reality.

This simple truth does not exclude Free Will. We are becoming more aware of just how much conscious control we have in the creation of our Reality. We either Consciously Create our experiences through the process of Manifestation or we attract the Energy that we are transmitting to The

Universe.

Before we have the Revelation of just how Peaceful our Awareness is, we realize how truly Powerful our Consciousness has always been. To better understand anything, we must give it our attention. If we wish to remain unaware of any concept, we are free to ignore it altogether. As funny as it might sound, hatred is the least amount of appreciation that one can offer to anything.

We deserve to feel however we believe and will experience exactly whatever we wish to feel. Whatever we believe that we do not deserve, we ignore completely. If we believe that God Loves us unconditionally, we deserve to feel that Love because we are Supremely Grateful. If we ignore the connection to The Soul, we believe we deserve to be punished and will feel disconnected because of how we feel about our past experiences. We are creating our suffering because we are judging God whenever we judge the experience in a manner that has zero degrees of appreciation.

When an occurrence can at the bare minimum gain our attention by causing us to hate it, we are beginning the assessment process. A judgment is a form of assessment, but it has a very minimal degree of appreciation. Any judgment that possesses hatred, disdain, disgust, or fear brings more of those emotions right back to the Being processing that information. As with all information presented to you, we are not supposed to ignore those Emotions. We are meant to learn from them. All Feelings are occurring for a reason. Emotions are very real and authentic in providing you with useful information. Acceptance of those disturbing Emotions allows the Being to become more aware of a lesson being taught. The lesson will be repeated until it is learned. When someone wonders why certain experiences continue to occur to them…this is the reason why.

If we can pay attention to something that we wish to better understand, even if that attention is that of hatred, we can begin to become more aware of that which has been presented to us. That hatred can turn into disgust but with a minimal degree of respect.

I had an experience 29 years ago. I was home from college on a summer break. My folks were away and I had free rein to do as I pleased. Well…I had left a turkey sandwich in a styrofoam container on the kitchen counter. I don't remember how long it had been sitting there, but I came across that turkey sandwich after a few days. I was compelled to open it, and lo and behold, guess what I saw? I saw a maggot-infested sandwich that just about made me vomit.

My lesson was simple…either refrigerate leftover food or discard it. Needless to say, I never made that mistake again. I believe that even though I was quite disgusted by what I saw, there must have been a minimal amount of respect for the common housefly. They can be viewed as pests. They are supposed to annoy you. They are begging you to clean up after yourself. They exist for one purpose...to continue the cycle of life. A fly is quite an amazing creature. It finds a way to survive. All insects, spiders, and worms find a way. Life finds a way. Respect all Life Forms.

When you can respect all Life Forms, allow yourself to respect every single experience that has ever occurred to you or will occur to you. Let your respect grow to appreciation and even gratitude. When you can at least respect everything, you have discovered purpose in that which you are discovering. This process of discovery is learning. The more you learn, the more aware you will become. With Awareness comes illumination. Enlightenment does one thing...it enables you to better understand why we are here on Earth.

BE GRATEFUL FOR LIFE
APPRECIATE ALL THINGS
RESPECT ALL PROCESSES

9. BEING A TRANSCEIVER

Every single particle that has ever existed is a transceiver. Light is the primary processing Energy Form. Through Time, the friction causes the transference of Energy to occur. The transference of Energy reforms the molecules and transforms matter from one state of being into another. These interactions between particles can be described by science as nuclear fusion, ionizations, and chemical reactions, but are all communications.

The connection of all things occurs on the Quantum level. Physicists enjoy speaking about Quantum Entanglement but are apprehensive about accepting the Spiritual nature of this connection. The barrier to better understanding anything is fear.

Full acceptance of such concepts as Quantum Entanglement includes all aspects of our states of being including the Spiritual aspect. Science accepts only observable evidence as being truthful. Natural philosophers review all information and assess its value from a level playing field. Every conceivable perspective is an equally valid perception. Because every single particle possesses a degree of Consciousness, all things are connected through this Intergalactic Conscious Web called Spirit. The Spirit cannot be observed, as it gives off no Electro-magnetic Radiation, but it can be felt.

Through this Spirit Connection, all particles communicate with other particles. All matter...all Beings are receiving Energetic Frequencies and transmitting them. These interactions do not cease through the course of that Being's evolutionary development. The existence in the Physical Realm is where all Beings learn how to process information.

Most Beings are unaware of just how vital they are in the Universe. They feel insignificant because they feel disconnected. When you are ignored, you tend to believe that you do not matter. You think that you have no control over your Reality when you have only to re-remember how to redevelop your Belief System.

As we become more aware of who and what we are, we are more readily able to accept why we are here. At a bare minimum, because of how Consciousness and Awareness work symbiotically, we are rediscovering just how useful everything is. Every thought we think of, a word spoken, an action taken, and an emotion felt serves not just *a purpose,* but The Highest Purpose! All things serve The Universe. Energy is continuously recycling and transforming from one state of being to another. All Things are Beings. All Beings are Transceivers.

Consciousness is expressed through the Universe. All Energy is reflected for more processing. Every single thing exists to receive Spirit Fuel and convert that from Electro-magnetic Energy to Physical Matter. Without the guidance of Spirit, our Energy Processing Plants stall out and become disrupted. The flow of energy becomes blocked, causing distress. These disturbances lead to stress on our various systems, which leads to diseases and illnesses.

When we can acknowledge our role in the Universe, we can view all processes from a new perspective. We are allowing ourselves to be willing participants in this process called Life. When we view any of the processes of life disrespectfully, we lose sight of the purpose of that process. This naturally occurs when we lose Faith in ourselves. When the belief in our abilities dwindles, we are less willing to be active participating members in life. When we doubt ourselves, that feedback maintains the very frequencies we think we do not want to experience any longer. These experiences are all lessons. We lather, rinse, and repeat over and over again until we cleanse our perception.

It is perfectly acceptable to be curious about whatever we are compelled to experience. As we become more aware of just how powerful we have always been, we can begin to alter our Consciousness by changing our perspective and refocusing our perception. As we reinterpret the purpose of any given process, we loosen up our judgment of that process. We accept that all experiences are intended as awareness lessons. We can learn something from every single experience that occurs to us. That is an exciting idea. With every lesson learned, we become more aware. We are becoming illuminated. We are becoming Human Beings.

BE AWARE OF EVERYTHING

ALLOW FOR ALL EXPERIENCES TO TEACH

LEARN FROM EVERYONE YOU ENCOUNTER

10. BECOMING A TRANSPONDER

Upon the expansion of our Awareness to be understanding of what we are, we become consciously aware of why we are here on Earth. All living beings and things are Transceivers whether they are aware of this state of being or not. Having this Realization places the Sentient Being in a position to take control of their conscious creativity.

We are becoming more aware of how to utilize Energy as information. As we learn how to more efficiently use Energy, we can pay attention to our Spirit Level. As we become more conscious of our Awareness, we are more ready to absorb information freely. The more information we absorb, the more aware we become. The more our Awareness expands, the more we realize how Peaceful we can feel. We have the Revelation that God's Will is for us to feel as Peaceful As God Feels.

The experience of feeling One with the Universe is an occurrence that is immeasurable. When this type of experience happens to us, thoughts and emotions occur along with these otherworldly feelings. We become compelled to share that feeling as we believe we are duty-bound to do so. These gifts of Awareness will be shared whether or not we are conscious of what is occurring. When we are sufficiently aware of how we feel, we have an innerstanding of the Universe of why it benefits all by consciously sharing this information.

We do not need to prove anything by sharing what we have learned. We do not *know anything* with 100% understanding. We can only share ways of perceiving that which cannot be fully understood and only experienced through feelings. We no longer need to fight or argue, as we feel peaceful beyond measure with whatever rate of Consciousness we are currently observing or level of Awareness we are feeling in the present moment of The Eternal Now.

We realize that we can consciously create any Reality we wish. The admission price is simple…

PAY ATTENTION TO
YOUR FEELINGS NOW!

I feel that this is not too much to ask. If you feel compelled to express yourself…do so without any fears, expectations, or assumptions. If you strongly believe that you are meant for something so great that if you were able to describe your Vision to others they may think you are crazy…have no fear. If you wish to feel only love and compassion for all, then simply appreciate all experiences. Respect every Being's right to believe what they will and their choice to think whatever they wish to think.

By practicing your Free Will, while not imposing your Will on others, you are consciously allowing others to experience their journey as they were meant to live it. You are allowing the free flow of information to be expressed by the Universe.

Whenever you fight or argue, your message will be unclear. When you are angry, frustrated, or confused, you are disturbed. These disturbances will distract you from The Message. There are plenty of disturbing thoughts that pop into our minds, emotions we may not like, or images that we see.

As we are illuminated, we are becoming more enlightened. This expansion of Awareness brings more clarity and insight to what we are feeling which further dissolves any toxicity that can build up if we ignore the Sines, Symbols, Signals, and Synchronicities. We can use any feeling as our Spirit Guides.

When something doesn't feel right, or it just seems off…we are supposed to question our beliefs. It is a more peaceful process to reshape your beliefs based on how you choose to feel than think you are right about something but feeling miserable. When you feel compelled to share some insight, knowledge, or information, it does not mean that you think you know something about a certain concept. Wishing to share wisdom because your understanding has allowed you to feel peaceful about a certain experience is being caring. This has nothing to do with the Ego or thinking you know something that others do not. Sharing your story because you believe it will shed light on a subject that others are also trying to better understand is the most compassionate act you can consciously perform. When you do these acts of kindness, you are spending your Time and Energy. When you do this of your own Free Will, without expectation of any reward, you are loving others unconditionally. By appreciating the process of discovery, you will find yourself paying attention to the present moment more frequently. By being present, your beliefs will maintain a degree of power as your imagination will be continuously fueled by inspirational ideas and feelings. You will feel more energetic and naturally freely exchange Energy by simply expressing yourself. Every intentional offering of truthful information will always refill The Spirit. You will find Peacefulness whenever you wish. You will go from being a Transceiver to a Transponder by consciously intending to share the message of truth and light.

BECOME A CONSCIOUS
TRANSPONDER BY
BEING AWARE

PART TWO

FREE THINKING

CHAPTER ONE

BEING FREE

1. IS EVERYTHING CONSCIOUS?

Two of the functions of Life are to respond to stimuli and transform Energy. This change in form can be considered as growth or development, which requires the processing of Energy. I contend that Energy is information that is utilized in the transformation of something that exists in Reality, from one state of being into another form of being.

Consciousness has three basic functions. Consciousness can create, perceive, and communicate. The Primary purpose of life is to process Energy. If Energy is information, then the transformation of Energy from one state of being to another is occurring for a reason. The cause of these transitions is due to changes in the frequency of Energy. Everything that has ever come into existence is becoming a currently existent thing, or will ever exist does so for a very specific reason or it would simply not occur.

If that thing can respond to any electromagnetic stimuli and react by changing the direction of its spin or position with the stimulating source, that something is conscious on a very basic level.

If an electron transitions from an excited state to a lower energy state, it gives off the equivalent amount of energy in the form of a photon. The photon becomes illuminated and is radiating. We can think of this expelling of energy as the cause of the motion of the electron back to its more familiar state of being. The effect of this reaction moves the electron back into its natural position.

If this scenario is accurate, the electron's expelling of energy is an expression of energy. The electron is consciously deciding when to move and takes action by creating a reaction called luminescence. In this scenario, the electron is exhibiting Consciousness on a very basic level.

Another possible explanation of what occurs during the process of luminescence is that the photon decides when the electron will move by expressing itself by radiating light. This expression of becoming illuminated is a signal, letting the electron know that it can move back into the home position. In this scenario, the photon is the shot-caller and a messenger of sorts. The photon is acting consciously. Its reaction of radiating is causing the electron to change its position.

A third possibility exists. The interaction between the electron and photon is a mutually agreed upon communication that results in each thing responding accordingly and doing exactly what it was meant to do. In this explanation, both things are conscious and have had an exchange of information. This interaction is a form of communication as two different things seemingly respond to the other.

A fourth possibility cannot be denied. The interaction is occurring by accident and is only a coincidence. Causality is not required for a coincidence to occur. Two things coinciding without a reason or a purpose seems highly improbable, although still within the realm of possibility.

Which of these scenarios makes the most sense to you? Which possibility is the most reasonable and logical depiction of what is occurring? Keep in mind that science can measure only that which can be observed through the naked eye or a tool that can capture electromagnetic radiation and store that information.

The effects of Consciousness can be observed by all Human Beings. The most obvious effect of Consciousness is what we call Reality. Side effects of Reality include other measurable things such as the alteration of brain waves. Consciousness itself, however, cannot be measured because it cannot be observed by anything.

Until we can somehow measure Consciousness, we can either accept that it exists in our Reality or deny that it exists. To deny that Consciousness exists is to deny our existence for we are Conscious Beings. I prefer to believe that I exist and coexist with all other Beings and Things. I choose to believe that this connection to all, on a Quantum level, includes All Things. The direct connection between All Things regardless of the level of Awareness or the rate of electromagnetic frequency is Consciousness. All Things are consciously being. All Beings are alive. Everything exists for a reason or they would not come into our Reality.

When we accept that there are processes that maybe we are not yet capable of understanding, and proceed on our journey anyway, we feel peaceful. That level of peace is determined by how much information we absorb and process, which infuses us with Light Form Energy. These infusions illuminate us and the Oscillating Rate of Conscious Frequency increases. This absorption of information clears up those matters that confuse us. With an increase in clarity, answers become more apparent. As we solve more and more riddles by finding answers to those questions, we become more powerful. This surge in power expands our Awareness. With this expansion, our feelings are intensified and we will become more peaceful.

We can maintain any frequencies we wish by sharing what we have learned with others. The only requirement for maintenance is to have as few expectations as possible. It is only human to assess our actions before we take them. The deeper lesson within each teaching becomes known as your Awareness expands and you pay attention to how you are feeling. Every thought, emotion, belief, and feeling has as deep of a lesson as we can wish to discover.

2. WHY DEATH IS NOT FINAL

Life is defined as the attributes of an organism or matter that includes a response to stimuli, a transformation of energy, and reproduction. Responding to stimuli is an interaction between a life form and Electro-magnetic Energy resulting in a reaction to information.

The transformation of energy includes types of metabolism such as absorption, excretion, and respiration, as well as reproduction. Metabolism is simply the occurrence of chemical reactions in living organisms required to sustain their life.

Absorption in animals is the obtaining of nutrients including the consumption of food and the breaking down of those nutrients into glucose to be used as a source of energy (digestion)

Plants absorb light and synthesize glucose from carbon dioxide and water producing oxygen. (photosynthesis). All living organisms require the absorption of water. Animals excrete carbon dioxide and waste materials including urine and feces.

Plants excrete excess carbon dioxide and oxygen.

Cellular Respiration, occurring in all life forms is the chemical reaction between oxygen and glucose and the excretion of carbon dioxide and water.

The action of reproduction does require that the organism responds to stimuli as well as the processing and transformation of energy, but not all things reproduce biologically. Replication, for example, can potentially occur with an Artificially Intelligent entity, but unless that process incorporates the utilization of Hydrogen, Oxygen, Nitrogen, and Carbon, it would not be considered alive in a biological sense.

All of these processes of life have one thing in common. This commonality is the conversion of energy from one form to another. These CONVERSIONS are CONVERSatIONS, which are simply exchanges of informatION. All forms of electromagnetic radiatION move. This motION occurs in IONizatIONS and chemical reactIONS. An ION is an atom or molecule that has an electrical charge caused by the loss or gain of one or more electrons. If you will kindly refer back to the First Law of Thermodynamics and realize that if energy cannot be destroyed, this simply means that it does not stop its motION. The IONS do not suddenly stop their primary behavior of moving and cease to exist.

What constitutes death?

If there is a breakdown in any of these life processes, then life will not proceed as it had the potential to do. If an animal does not get enough food or water, it will die. If there is a drought and plants do not get sufficient water, they will die. If a human drowns and cannot breathe, it will die. With the passing of any life form, the process of dying is not final. If plants or animals contract a virus, the plant or animal can exhibit symptoms from types of disease and can die.

A new process occurs when any living organism dies. This process is called decompositION. This process includes the breakdown of matter. Bacteria and fungi utilize the plant or animal matter that has died as food. The breaking down of this matter results in the opposite of chemical synthesis. More complex compounds are reduced to more simple compounds that are more useful as they exist in a state of being that will be easily synthesized by plants and animals.

Think of the most complicated word you can imagine. I was going to use Supercalifragilisticexpialidocious, which has 34 letters, but I looked up the longest word in the English language which is

Pneumonoultramicroscopicsilicovolcanoconiosis, which has 45 letters. One word I can say while the other just seems like it isn't worth the effort. Both words possess several of the 26 letters in the English alphabet. Both have one-word synonyms. Although one can make a case for it being unnecessary to use the full version, it is certainly fun saying supercalifragilisticexpialidocious. I suppose saying that other word could be fun, but I will most likely never bother trying.

My point is that the learning process can become too confusing when the information seems too complicated. If we break down the material into bite-size pieces that are more digestible, the learning process is more enjoyable and becomes fun.

The same thing applies to the processes of biology. Chemical bonding in biology most easily occurs using the four foundational elements of life: Hydrogen, Oxygen, Nitrogen, and Carbon. The most important chemical reactions incorporate simple compounds such as H^2O (water), CO^2 (carbon dioxide), NH^3 (ammonia), and CH^4 (methane).

Let's begin by acknowledging that Life has no opposite. The previously understood dichotomy of Life and Death is an oppositional way of viewing each. Although it is understandable and even reasonable to perceive these two concepts as being opposing forces, let's begin with the most open-minded premise of accessing knowledge and allowing ourselves to believe that anything is possible.

Let us acknowledge that the one thing that all Life Forms have in common is that they possess Energy. What do we accept as true as it pertains to the study of Energy? If we understand how The First Law of Thermodynamics and $E=mc^2$ work together, and accept that the Absolute Duality of The Universe is being Energy≈Spirit, then we can feel very peaceful that nothing ever actually dies and is only transformed.

Allow me to elaborate further. The First Law of Thermodynamics states that energy is neither created nor destroyed but only changes in form. This means that energy is neither born into a living state of being nor does it cease to exist. What occurs to energy when it transforms? It changes its rate of frequency. This change is equivalent to a change in its motion. If our motion dictates our level of energy, the faster we move, the more energy is generated.

If a physical body transforms from one state of being to another, it transfers the energy from certain frequencies to new ones. This energy is the exact informatION that allows for the processing to continue. Nothing ceases to exist or stops moving for eternity.

EVERYTHING MATTERS
ENERGY FORMS MATTER
LIFE IS ETERNAL

3. RATIONAL AND REAsonabLe REALity

Each being spends their time existing in their REALity. As we are being aware of our Consciousness while becoming conscious of our Awareness, we REALize that our beliefs are as REAL as we allow them to be. We can resonate with others who have similar beliefs because we share a similar level of understanding about whatever topic we are discussing. When we have a shared understanding, this is because the information that was provided to both beings made sense.

All beliefs are rational. The idea of something being irrational is understandable but is somewhat misleading. The only thing that makes sense regarding the aspect of irrationality is numbers. An irrational number is a real number that cannot be expressed as a simple fraction. A fraction is a ratio, hence the name RATIOnal. Irrational numbers such as π are always Transcendental. Irrational numbers make sense and are therefore within our range of understanding. Anything that becomes understandable falls within our scope of reason. Irrational numbers are reasonable.

Any concept that is not a number is incapable of being irrational because to be irrational is to be without ratio and is therefore immeasurable. Other synonyms for irrational include invalid and illogical. Just because something is immeasurable, this does not mean it cannot be understood to any degree. To dismiss something as being invalid is to place a limit on it by ignoring anything about it that can be understood. To believe that something is illogical is reasonable because you are understanding that it has no measurable aspect.

When someone says *"seeing is believing..."* this phrase makes sense because it is understandable and quite reasonable why they think in this manner. Logical thinkers use reasonable information to verify the truth. Empirical thought requires evidence provided by our senses to prove the validity of the theory. Many scientists claim to be logical but are empirical as they require observable evidence to verify a claim about something.

There is irony in one who claims to use logic but requires empirical evidence to validate something as true. The humorous part of these thinkers is that they only use observable evidence and refute those senses, which are more of a Spiritual nature.

We are conditioned to believe only what we can see or hear. We are discouraged to believe our other senses. It becomes irrational to believe those "other" feelings. We are told to stop being so emotional or not be hysterical. We are also taught that having irrational fears are just a sign that we have a mental disorder or that we are even possibly insane. These labels make sense to us and we are so conditioned by fear that we believe the validity of these possibilities and put our emotions in check.

I am purely logical because I absorb all available data and utilize all of my senses to feel everything. My thoughts pass through both hemispheres of my brain and I filter through the corrupted data and absorb the truthful information. All energy is useful, however, as sometimes I learn what not to think, say, or do.

To say that my or someone's beliefs, actions, or words are irrational or unreasonable is equivalent to saying or thinking that that being's beliefs, actions, or words are unreal. The number of humans who believe in the existence of anything directly correlates to how much sense it makes to those who are experiencing that occurrence.

Someone who is blind, for example, cannot see the Sun, and cannot hear the Sun. Why do they believe that the Sun exists? They grew up learning how to use all of their senses to gather information about the Sun. This included hearing about the Sun's existence, touching the description in Braille, and feeling the heat from the Sun on their skin. All of the information was processed in their Consciousness, and at some point, they chose to believe that Sun exists. This belief is perfectly rational and reasonable. You would have much difficulty discovering someone who does not believe that the Sun exists. The beautiful part about believing in anything is that one does not need to fully know how it works before forming whatever degree of belief you allow yourself to have. You are also welcome to modify your belief to larger degrees as you become more aware of how that thing functions and the purpose it serves.

The same logic applies to things of a Spiritual nature. Why are the concepts that have no observable proof such heated topics? If something cannot be measured, even though it cannot be seen, it does not mean it cannot be experienced on another level. Each Consciousness experiences its unique Reality that often has sympathetic frequencies that resonate with other beings. Those resonant frequencies harmonize because they feel peaceful and make sense. The more sense something makes, the more understandable it becomes, causing it to be very reasonable and therefore more widely accepted as occurring.

Many misunderstand the notion of there being only one Reality. There are an infinite array of realities within One Actuality. Don't worry...this has nothing to do with anything that you believe in because your Reality can be whatever you wish it to be. To refute another being's reality as being true is to refute their belief system as being valid.

To dispel another being's beliefs is to dispel an aspect of their being. In a way, you are dispelling that being and casting a spell denying that they are a part of their existence.

I believe in the MAGIcal powers of rainbows to spark our iMAGInations. I believe in the healing powers of laughter. I believe that Love is all we ever truly need to Thrive. How do you feel about this vision of Reality? Does it make sense and feel peaceful, or does it seem confusing in any manner?

It doesn't matter what you believe in as long as you always believe in yourself.

4. I AM AWARE

We spend much of our lives experiencing countless occurrences trying to figure out who and what we are.

After going through these processes of living, we begin to think that we know who and what we are. We often get ahead of ourselves and attempt to better understand why we are here, before getting a handle on who and what we are. I have found that trying to understand the why, before accepting the who and what can lead to much confusion.

As soon as we are blessed with believing in ourselves, we begin to have a deeper understanding of why we are here. This level of Awareness is expanded through many experiences that involve deep feelings. Depending on what we believe about ourselves, we will feel however we deserve to feel about how much we accept ourselves. One of the hardest things to do while processing the information that is provided to us is to love ourselves unconditionally.

All learning occurs whether we realize it or not. Learning is simply the receiving of information, processing that energy, and storing the data as memory imprints. Regardless of how much of the information is accepted as truth, it is all useful in determining the only thing that ever really matters. That one thing that matters the most is how we feel in any given moment of Awareness.

The idea that people are asleep and therefore need to wake up is understandable but shows a lack of Awareness of any who hold this belief. This is only an assessment based on my understanding of Awareness. Just like there are infinite degrees of Consciousness, there are infinitely expanding Spheres of Awareness.

Each of us has our earliest memory of an occurrence that can be described as a Spiritual Awakening. For the longest time, my earliest memory was when I was three years old. My twin brother poked me in my left eye with a toy gun. I remember no pain but experienced a spike in the Awareness of my Sense of Sight, Smell, Motion, and the power of emotions such as compassion. My first thoughts immediately after the immediate surge of energy resulted in an instant increase in the rate of my Consciousness. What followed within seconds was the feeling of Awareness of my compassion. My first realization was that my parents were extremely stressed out and frantic. I wanted to comfort them.

I remember seeing my first color being the purple/maroon hue of the shirt my dad wore. I remember driving to the hospital and looking out of the window. The next thing I remember was being wheeled on the gurney on the way to the surgical room. I was feeling super high and loved that sensation of moving. Lastly, before going under, I remember smelling the anesthesia gas. It was a sickly aroma. Despite what was occurring throughout this experience, I was quite peacefully aware. I had no fear, no feelings other than compassion, and the sensations of Sight, Motion, and Smell. I don't remember hearing, touching, tasting, or sensing Space or Time during this event in my life.

Years later, maybe around the age of 20, I found a photo of our 3rd birthday party. My mom and dad got us each a cake. Mine was green and Pat's was blue if I remember correctly. The photo was taken from our kitchen, pointing toward our dining room. I haven't looked at the photo since then, but I seem to remember Patrick on my left behind the dining room table with our cakes on the table and both of us giving the thumbs-up sign. As I saw the cakes, I had a vision of what became my actual earliest memory, which occurred as I viewed the cake with the candles lit. Time stood still as I viewed the three candles. I don't remember seeing my mom, dad, or Patrick. It is just now dawning on me that they would have been singing the happy birthday song as this is the tradition, but I don't remember experiencing any other Sense other than Sight but felt so much love and joy. I am tearing up just thinking about how grateful I was to have such loving parents and an awesome brother. My brother and I were adopted by Jesse and Wilma Evrard in 1970. I don't remember when I became aware of this piece of information, but I don't remember anything other than what that meant from a biological perspective.

From a Spiritual aspect, I just knew that my mom and dad loved us very much. Anyway...going back to this magical moment in time is my earliest memory. I remember seeing the cake before the candles were lit. It was a Cowboy and Native American Indian motif with little plastic figures and it had green icing. The next thing I was aware of was seeing the three candles having been lit. I then was frozen in time viewing the flame of the middle candle. Several seconds lasted for an Eternity as I became one with the flame. The colors of blue, orange, and yellow danced right before my eyes. I often wondered what 20/20 vision would look like after sustaining damage to my cornea. Well...my vision at age 3 was a perfect 20/20, one in which I saw all that I needed to know to become fully aware of who and what I was. I knew then and there that everything was going to be truly beautiful. I experienced Consciousness and Awareness and had only a feeling of Peacefulness.

I spent the years 3-50 living a wonderful life filled with a whole range of experiences ranging from beautifully joyful to disturbingly tormenting. Thankfully, most of my childhood, from 3-17, was wonderful and amazing. My parents gave us many opportunities to experience things such as sports, Boy Scouts, and playing musical instruments. I did have OCD and ADHD but was never officially diagnosed with those, so I just had to adjust. In junior high, I began having bouts of depression. From 16-27, I began to party, experienced sexual abuse, drug abuse, jail, living on the streets, and had some very dark depression. This was very much a rollercoaster of blissful highs to horrible lows. I would not change even one second of any of these experiences. Because of the variety and range of degrees of emotions that I felt, I can better understand why people do what they do.

The entire time from 3-50, I was aware of everything that was occurring to me. I was conscious of my thought process and belief system. I was conscious of my 5 Basic Senses and felt my emotions deeply. I was aware of my Three States of Being (Physical, Mental, and Emotional). I was conscious of my Spirituality and did not allow any to dispel how I viewed God, including the Presbyterian church we attended. I questioned everything, especially that whole concept of going to Hell for Eternity. I simply refused to comply with the belief that a loving God would ever punish any being by damning them to Hell for even a little while. I held to my beliefs and my understanding of God. I kept my Faith through it all.

I was always aware of how I felt about everything, especially how people viewed me and what I believed they thought about me. I was never comfortable in my skin until I began accepting everything about myself starting April 12, 2020. This was Easter Sunday, and even though I didn't go to a traditional church, I prayed to God that I was ready to seek the truth. I was open to diving deep and took the opportunity during the Covid shutdowns to do some Soul searching.

I learned how our Consciousness is Who we are, while Awareness is What we are. Consciousness receives Energy through our Senses, processes it, and relays that information to the Awareness. Our Awareness is how we feel about whatever we experience in the Reality of our Consciousness. We are all in the same Ocean of Awareness, each perceiving and believing whatever we wish so that life makes sense. We are all becoming more aware at different rates of conscious frequency and expanding our Awareness to different levels. We are all already awake, for we have never actually fallen completely asleep.

I AM AWARE OF
BECOMING MORE
AWARE EVERY MOMENT
I FEEL CONSCIOUSLY ALIVE

5. THE NOTION OF MOTION

The one thing that everything possesses is the actION of motION. The idea or notION of motION is simple. Anything that comes into existence can only be a thing if it moves. Nothing that has ever occurred, whether it exists in the Physical or Spiritual REALm became what it was, is, or will be without the act of moving.

What is motion?

MotION is the observable change of positION through Space over a perIOd of Time. We can see how motIOn is measured on an XY graph. As with all forms of measurement, we use the concept of numbers to describe the coordinates that show the changes that occur.

Motion becomes the observable evidence of something existing in REALity. Science is the study of the behavior of all forms of Energy. All things are in a constant state of flux. Since $E=mc^2$, all things presented in the Physical REALm are moving on a macro, micro, or quantum level. In short, science is the study of the act of moTION. Nothing is perfectly still except for the Void of Nothingness within the Spiritual REALm, but even that absence of light, silence, and lack of motion is only temporary.

The factor that distinguishes one thing from another is the Rate of

Oscillation called frequency. The rate is the measurement of the change of direction of a wave for one second known as hertz (Hz). Each measurable frequency has a distance of this movement called the wavelength.

All things exhibit characteristic behaviors, which are nothing more than the interactions and reactions between two or more pieces of matter. The ability to move is the one thing that everything that ever comes into existence shares with everything else that has ever existed or will ever exist. There is a chain of events that have been occurring, are occurring, and will continue to occur for Eternity. These events are a series of cause-and-effect occurrences. Every single event that occurs to every quantum of Energy shares one thing in common during its existence, it changes its position in the Space-Time Continuum (motion).

Space serves as the Zeroth Dimension for anything to come into being. Any state of being is Divinely inspired and begins with being able to be observed by other beings. Anything that is yet to be observed temporarily remains waiting to become an existent thing. The Spiritual State of Being, which is yet to be, occurs before becoming something within the Physical REALm.

The first state of being is that which requires to be observed. This initial requirement is the First Dimension of Light. Without light, nothing can be seen. Nothingness is all that there would be in the absence of Electromagnetic-Energy and no things would be able to be observed in the Physical REALm. Without the ability to be observed, there is no means to begin an exchange of energy. Electromagnetism occurs because heat is sensed. The most basic type of interaction between particles is the exchange of energy called induction. This form of communication causes motion to occur.

For particles to be able to receive the communication as a Light Form, being that there are no eyes with which to see, the waveform is felt. That which causes the waveform to move is the Second Dimension of Sound. Particles interpret the data through the Sense of Sound because it is felt. Music has the power to make you want to take part in the act of physically moving your body called dancing because it affects your eMOTIONs. If you hear live music or dance music from powerful speakers, those thumping bass frequencies are felt in your chest and alter your heart rate.

The visible light spectrum is available for living organisms to receive energy, absorb it, process it, and transform that energy into various metabolic functions. All forms of metabolism cause cells to react through motion. Light Forms and Sound Forms are the two foundations of communication between all things. Higher rates of Consciousness can interpret faster rates of frequencies including more complex Light Forms known as the written language. All beings feel various degrees of energy and even basic life forms can sense when interactions are occurring. The most basic signal is to turn it on. The next higher order of a signal is to move. The First State of Being is to exist. This is something having a switch flipped to the on position. To exist is to simply Be. A thing's first actION in its existence is that of illuminatION. The Universe knows when this occurs through that being having possessed its ability to be observed. The Second State of Being is becoming. A being becomes more functional with its second act of existence, which is that of motION.

The freedom to move is the Divine Right shared by every single thing that exists in the Physical REALm. To impede another being or thing from being able to perform the motion that it was specifically created to perform is an imposition of the highest magnitude. Imagine being denied your ability, which allows you to function as you are genetically designed to do. To enslave another is to restrict one's ability to move freely.

Motion is the one thing that allows the Universe to continue to exist. Motion causes all things to occur in the Universe. For humans to become more knowledgeable, our Consciousness becomes more powerful by increasing its rate of frequency. We can become perfectly still by simply being silent. Here we no longer feel the need to move because we have already found our way home.

This Zero Point is the actual ON positiON. Time and Space, become felt in their Infinite States of Being... perfectly still and deadly silent. The need for Motion becomes temporarily unnecessary.

6. WHAT DOES IT MEAN TO FORGIVE?

To forgive is to bless another with the gift of understanding. When we are angry with someone, we think that we are angry at them because of something they did or said. In some cases, we are jealous of the one with whom we are mad. The truth is that we are upset with ourselves for secretly wishing that we could do what another dared to do.

In most cases, whenever we are triggered, we are being judgmental. The level of hatred or condemnation is commensurate with the degree of misunderstanding. Those horrific acts that seemingly make absolutely no sense simply do not register with our ability to conceive why anyone could even consider doing that level of harm to another.
We cannot comprehend ourselves taking that action and cannot understand how another can perform such an act.

The reason we cannot seem to understand the other being's actions is that we simply do not know their history. We have no idea what sort of experiences must have occurred to them that might begin to explain their frame of mind. The 2017 film *The Shack* does a masterful job of describing what forgiveness is, and how it heals those who suffer in any manner.

When we deny the truth of anything, we feel pain. When we accept the truth of whatever we are in the process of better understanding, we are set free of the burden of judgment.

The miracle of life is that we are not only allowed to better understand God, but we are also genetically engineered to know as much about God as we wish to know. The only thing that is required of us to do is have Faith. As long as we are breathing, we are existing. We would not exist for no reason at all. We exist for the highest purpose. As we rediscover why we are here on Earth, we are experiencing everything that is meant to occur to us for the same reason that anything occurs.

As we become more aware of how things work, we seem to become more conscious of how to use our Awareness to increase our rate of Consciousness. As we allow ourselves to become more informed, we absorb more Energy from the Electromagnetic Spectrum. EM radiation does the one thing it was designed to do...it illuminates our light-gathering bodies. Our Mental, Physical, and Emotional States of Being are all being utilized in the transformation of this information into other forms of energy that are used to manifest Reality into our existence. When we gather information from all of our senses, we expand our Awareness by simply feeling our way through these denser fields of Energy.

The hardest thing for humans to understand is why suffering exists at all.

We want to believe in God and would rather be God-loving beings than God-fearing ones. To have the levels of Faith required to transcend, we patiently allow for our life process to occur.

All humans are blessed with exactly the experiences that are necessary to get their attention. Upon the recognition of that which is occurring, we become present in our Awareness and pay attention to how we feel. When we deny these feelings, we remain at the same level of Awareness as when were conscious of our Reality. Having Faith is trusting that the entire process is intended for our development. We are not required to like every single moment of each experience that occurs to us. We just have to respect the whole process.

If we truly wish to increase our knowledge regarding anything, we can begin with a better understanding of God. To know why we are here on Earth currently begins with accepting what we are. To understand what we are, it is imperative to know who we are. As you become more aware of who you are, you will believe in yourself no matter what has occurred to you during your life experiences. As you accept who you are, everything becomes more apparent to you, and your Awareness of what you become evident. Knowing what you allow you to feel everything. When you utilize more of your senses, everything simply makes more sense because there is less and less confusion, doubting, and misinterpretations. Your reason for being will become crystal clear.

The entire process of self-discovery is facilitated through the act of forgiveness. Each being we forgive is a form of meditation that allows us to practice the act of forgiving others. Each being we forgive is an act of kindness. Every single time we share love unconditionally, we reveal who we are by accepting what we are. The more we practice this art form, the more creative we become and the more we discover that judging any of our life processes is also going to feel like a burden. When we judge anything, we are judging The One, for it is through God, The Creator, that anything exists.

We have heard the phrase *"God works in mysterious ways."* If we accept that all things serve a purpose, including the process of suffering, we will be provided many experiences through which we may practice our Faith. If we trust the process, and we do so without any expectations or attachment to anything, we remain faithful. We are not only allowed to know the answers to everything we wish to better understand, I feel that God provides us with all of our experiences to test our Faith.

I feel that God loves us perfectly. To love another perfectly is to love without condition. How can God love us unconditionally but feel the need to test our Faith? If God is Omniscient, is it not possible that God knows what is best for us? The answers to every question you ever had or will possibly wish to know are within you.

KNOW MORE THROUGH
FEELING EVERYTHING

7. SYMbioticSYMphony

Everything is connected. Physicists study our physical reality by observing how electromagnetic energy moves, and how matter interacts with other pieces of energy and changes its frequency. All sciences measure various types of matter, life forms, and the processing of energy. We accept what we can observe because seeing is believing. The best explanation of our Physical Realm appears to currently be Quantum Entanglement.

A Spiritual Being studies how our spiritual experiences give our life meaning. We are becoming more aware of how to tap into those otherworldly feelings. When we trust our feelings such as intuition, we are aware of great change that is about to occur. We store the information about the experience in our memory data banks for retrieval to be utilized as a teachable lesson. Upon reconciliation of the processing of Energy, the information becomes knowledge. If we share that knowledge, it becomes wisdom.

Being a natural philosopher, one can gather information from all sources. It does not matter if we seek to know more about science, nature, spirituality, religion, or faith-based ideologies. If you have ever wondered how things work and sought out the answers to those questions, you are being philosophical. If you learn how something functions, or why it exists, and it makes sense to you, that information was absorbed into your mind. You have become more illuminated. Your Oscillating Rate of Conscious Frequency has increased because you have accepted that data as truthful. If you allow yourself to take that knowledge and feel it, your Awareness expands.

As we learn more about anything that we study, we feel compelled to express our feelings in various art forms, including playing music, singing, dancing, painting, drawing, sculpting, doing pottery, taking photographs, or writing poetry. Expressing how we feel is a beautiful way to give of ourselves. Sharing freely is a generous way to show kindness toward others.

Whenever we find ourselves confused or doubting ourselves, we have access to a true blessing whenever we wish. The one thing that we all are capable of appreciating if nothing else is Mother Nature. When all else fails, our ability to breathe fresh air will allow us to feel alive. We are not required to understand how we breathe in nitrogen, oxygen, and trace amounts of other elements, or that we exhale carbon dioxide that plants use in combination with minerals and water from the soil in conjunction with light to convert the water and carbon dioxide molecules into glucose. The plants release their byproduct of oxygen. Our basic function of respiration is dependent on a perfectly designed and symBIOtic symphony in which all BIOlogical organisms function with each other, including fungi, bacteria, and even viruses.

If we appreciate all of these symphonies of energy that occur in our lives, we will feel peaceful. Understanding these processes is not required, but super fun if you enjoy the art of discovery. We will encounter incredibly irritating experiences. There will be things that we simply will not like and even find utterly disgusting. We will be uncomfortable as we process all of this information. We will feel real pain from an ouch to a "Holy Mother of God!" type of pain. Whenever we process that type of information, we always become more aware. We grow through these experiences if we absorb the information and transform that energy into something beautiful. Respect Mother Earth. She will provide you with all that you need... Hydrogen, Oxygen, Nitrogen, and Carbon.

FIND THE BEAUTY IN ALL AND DISCOVER ITS PURPOSE.

THE UNIVERSE FEELS YOUR APPRECIATION AND BLESSES YOU WITH PEACEFULNESS.

8. DECEIVING BELIEVERS

The act of deception is a powerful tool used to manipulate thoughts. All thoughts matter because they are the fundamental elements utilized in the formation of ideas. These ideas can turn into visions, which over time, can become manifestations of one's Reality. If you intentionally discourage another, you are deceiving them because their truth is their Reality.

The manifestation of a conscious frequency into the Physical Realm is determined by that conscious will if it is powerful enough to achieve the entropy of singularity. In other words...the dream has to be a believable story to ever really occur. If the storyteller does not believe their own story, they are less apt to tell their history. If they are afraid to tell their story, it may never be spelled out or become an incantation.

There are two types of Human Beings, with an infinite array of conscious frequencies. Some belief only what they see as their Reality and others know how to feel about the Actuality of their existence. This is simply an honest assessment that allows one to be able to decipher information that a being provides as they express themselves freely.

Accepting that some will inspire and others will deceive is also a recognition of truth. We may or may not know the other being's intentions, as more often than not, we know not their experiences. Instead of judging one another, we can assess the information that each one transmits and determine its value to our current existence.

"Adapt what is useful, reject what is useless, and add what is specifically your own." -Bruce Lee

Upon the recognition of Light Being the Source of Truth, we are more readily able to accept data from all of our experiences and learn from the information that is being received. The more Energy one absorbs through their whole body, the more information can be transformed into knowledge.

Through the transformation of Energy in Motion (E-Motion), we become more illuminated and our Awareness expands.

Our only disabilities are self-imposed. When we doubt ourselves, we generate thought patterns and emotions of shame, and guilt that causes us to be anxious. We become attached to these ideas of self-loathing and fall back to our victim role. No one claims that the journey is easy. It is painful, treacherous, difficult, and confusing. As we move into our true selves, however, life becomes fun, joyful, and pleasurable again...just like when we were three years old.

As you become more aware of what you are and why you are here, everything becomes clearer. You will continue to encounter the deceivers...those who will intentionally attempt to crush your Spirit. Guess what happens to those poor in Spirit? They fail miserably and wind up living in fear.

My hope for all seekers of truth is that they learn how to believe in themselves by trusting their intuition while they gather information from all experiences. Every interaction in life is an opportunity to learn more. There are no limits to what you can know. Even those experiences that occur, in which another is trying to deceive you, can be a teachable moment. Sometimes the lesson is simply what not to do.

You will know when another is lying to you. It doesn't matter when you have that revelation. Don't bother feeling ashamed for being duped. Your experience will make you more aware. You will have fine-tuned your intuition and that next deceiver will be felt. Keep an open mind each time you are tricked or fooled, and instead of judging yourself harshly, form a memory that will be recalled at the perfect moment in time. The time for discernment is always crucial, for we can become jaded. This is understandable, but we can still learn something from everyone. Loving ourselves unconditionally is paramount in all of these experiences.

NEVER STOP BELIEVING IN YOURSELF.

KEEP THE FAITH AND LOVE ALL UNCONDITIONALLY.

9. THINKING, BELIEVING, FEELING

I strongly feel that there are different degrees of knowing. We can know anything, but we often misunderstand which degree of knowledge we currently are. Knowing anything is simply a matter of understanding. Words matter, so don't be surprised if you claim to possess a certain level of understanding and another being misunderstands what you are saying and possibly misinterprets your intentions.

All levels of knowledge are acceptable. All misunderstandings arise from assumptions as to what others think, believe, or feel. Assumptions are simply claims of a certain degree of knowing something that is yet to be known. Whenever you think you know something before having the level of understanding that equates to your claim, you will very likely come off as insincere.

For example, when you try to console another being upon the passing of a loved one, and you use the phrase "I know how you feel..." you will sound like you know what you are talking about if you have felt that type of pain because you have gone through a similar occurrence. If you say that same phrase before actually feeling what it is like, you might mean well, but will not come across as being sincere because your level of understanding about what that experience feels like is not as deep as the one who has gone through that experience.

In this situation, consider saying something such as..."I can only begin to imagine..." or "I cannot fathom how painful this is."

By saying these types of phrases, you are showing that you care while being honest about your feelings. The being with whom you are communicating will feel your sincerity.

I believe that if you think you know something and accept that your level of knowledge about something is of a basic level, others will likely receive your comments well. When discussing what you are thinking, your level of Awareness is only at a basic level. If you make a statement with just a basic understanding of the concept or occurrence, being calm and employing a matter-of-fact cadence in your voice will further the conversation. If you are angry, resentful, bitter, or aggressive while describing your thoughts of something when your understanding is only on a basic level, you will come across as being a know-it-all, or quite ignorant. The number of misunderstandings will rise in conjunction with the level of assumptions that occur during conversations. All assumptions ever accomplished are breakdowns in the communication between the participants of the conversation.

I feel that the next level of knowledge is in the believing range. In this range of believing, your understanding of the topic of discussion is higher than that of the thinking range. When you believe in something, your Awareness about that topic is typically higher. This increase in Awareness is due to how you choose to perceive your experiences leading up to the conversation that brings to mind your beliefs. Our Belief System is based upon a combination of experiences, emotions felt during those occurrences, and the thought process you utilize to receive the information and transform that data. Statements like..."I believe that..." are going to carry more emotional content. Your voice will be higher pitched perhaps, and your volume may be louder but not too loud. Chances are, you will be spirited while remaining civil. Many beings still think that using the "I know..." phrase is useful when their understanding is only in the believable range. Often discussions of a Spiritual nature occur with one or more participants in the conversations about your beliefs. Any conversation regarding our Belief System will proceed beautifully until a participant in the conversation tries to dispel another's beliefs in any manner. Has anyone in the history of human beings able to speak or write ever been able to change the mind of another by telling them that their beliefs are wrong or even harmful to others? I tend to think that the answer to this question is no. Our strongly held beliefs are caused by the Realizations that occur when we observe connections between two things that were not previously thought of as being related.

The highest levels of knowing anything seem to occur when we use more of our senses to feel the information. We can see observable evidence that is real while feeling Spiritual occurrences at the same time. Whenever we have a Revelation, we combine two or more of our senses to be able to relate to the information. When someone says something that resonates with us, we say things like"That makes sense." More often than not, we see, hear, and feel in our hearts the truth in what is being experienced.

We become very passionate when we feel something in every fiber of our being. We are compelled to share what we have discovered because of how great it makes us feel.

When we learn to not make assumptions, have no expectations, and simply love one another, we become more aware of all of our experiences. This expansion in Awareness occurs when we become more knowing. I feel very strongly that all Human Beings can become more knowing if they are open-minded, and have a free Spirit and loving heart.

I AM KNOWING HOW TO BECOME MORE AWARE
BY FEELING EVERYTHING.

10. HOW DO YOU KNOW WHEN YOU KNOW?

There are different levels of knowing. We can think we know something. We think our thoughts, which are based on concepts that seem to pop into our mind from nowhere (now here). That nowhere is also known as our subconscious mind. Our initial thought forms are opinions, which are a type of belief. You know what they say about opinions...

Thoughts can cause us to feel a variety of emotions that are useful in giving meaningful content to those thoughts. Our thoughts can trigger emotions. The emotions make the experience real enough that they gain our attention. The more intense the emotion, the more indicative that there will be significant information that will be available for us to learn. All that is required to learn from those thoughts is paying attention to how we feel about the emotions in that present moment. The emotional content of these thoughts is the indicator of specific lessons that will eventually be learned or temporarily disregarded and ignored. If we judge the thought and ignore how we feel, we discount a part of the entire informational download.

We know the most accurate information during our present moments of Awareness. With certain ways of thinking, we can use our Conscience to filter information and disseminate what is right or wrong. This type of determination of the value of an information set is simple and effective. It is also limiting, as all prejudice before the point of absorption acts in the same fashion as resistors limit the flow of electricity in electronic equipment. If we learn how to rewire our brains to utilize greater capacity, we are reconnecting our built-in capacitors called neurons. We better understand things when this process occurs and we can say we have higher levels of knowledge because our Consciousness is oscillating at faster rates of frequency.

With faster rates of Consciousness comes more clarity. We use our belief system to maintain certain frequencies as we are processing information through our Imagination. We add more emotional content, and imagery from memories to enhance the movie that we are producing in our mental construct called the mind. It seems that all there is occurs in our Consciousness.

How do we know what is real? Simple...everything that you feel is a manifestation of your Reality. There are currently 8 billion different conscious realities all occurring at different rates of frequency. They all possess different degrees of truth and are only partially true. There is an Absolute Truth, but that is fully known, felt, and completely understood by The One.

So how does one even know if there is an afterlife, or if God exists, or that Love is not just a chemical reaction that induces the release of oxytocin? We know all of these things and everything based on how we feel about it as we are gathering information about that which we are studying. As our Belief System grows through the reformation of our beliefs that are formed through our thought process, we become more aware of how to use our feelings to better understand our thoughts that generate emotions that drive the whole process of manifestation of Spirit into our existence into whatever form we envision in our conscious minds.

I am beginning to wonder if thoughts are felt, which causes us to think more deeply about something we are contemplating, or if our feelings are thought of, which creates more things such as emotions. I suppose that it does not matter. What does matter is how we are feeling currently.

If we think we know something, but it is only an opinion, we are more apt to try to prove ourselves right whenever we are triggered by another. If we know that we may not know anything sufficiently, and to provide valuable information to others, we would be wise to pay attention to others who just might know a thing or two about the subject, we become truly ready to know more. Would you rather be able to learn more about something and become more peacefully aware, or think that you know something, before obtaining ALL of the potential information, and remain miserable?

Consciousness: How does one know anything?
Awareness: When do you feel it?

Consciousness: I mean...if the information is true?
Awareness: It's all partially true.

Consciousness: What if you become aware that the one with whom you are communicating is lying?
Awareness: All information, regardless of intent, is always partially true.

Consciousness: Is all information useful to me?
Awareness: All information is potentially beneficial, so yes...it's all useful.

Consciousness: How do you know which information I should pay attention to?
Awareness: By how it feels. Trust your intuition while being fearless.

Consciousness: So...what you are saying is that I determine the amount of information that I wish to accept?
Awareness: That is a great question, perhaps my favorite so far in this conversation. Yes...you control the show by dictating the flow of electricity.

Consciousness: So...let me get this straight...I am in total control of my capacitors and resistors?
Awareness: Yes. Any more questions?

Consciousness: Not at this point in time.

KNOWLEDGE SEEMS POWERFUL,
WHILE WISDOM FEELS PEACEFUL.

11. SEEING IS BELIEVING WHILE FEELING BECOMES KNOWING

Do you believe everything you see? I am always ready to believe anything I see. I understand that Reality is an illusion. An illusion does one thing incredibly well...it gains your attention. Many view illusion as a type of deception. You may equate illusion with being fooled.

When you see a magician perform their tricks, if you feel like you are being had, then you are missing the point of the illusion of magic. We think these acts in which these artists levitate can't be happening before our eyes, but there it occurs right in front of us. Are we not amazed? Do we not gasp in awe? We are amazed and even laugh out loud while we enjoy the show. The magician has done it once again...they have not only gained your attention, they have held your gaze to the point of time being temporarily irrelevant. Did not the show happen? Of course, it did. The actual magic was that you believed that action was possible. You didn't change your entire Belief System; you modified your beliefs about another's abilities. If only for a relatively short duration of Time, you believed that anything is possible. After all...life is designed to be fun.

Our Belief System is the driving force of our Imagination. During our childhood, we are truly gifted with vivid imaginations. We eventually became adults and may have been discouraged from believing in fantastical ideas such as unicorns and fairies. As we figure out that we determine our Reality, we re-remember how to be as we were as children.

What did we do better than anything else as children? Did we not feel everything deeply? If we were filled with joy, we laughed out loud. When we were truly frustrated, we had a tantrum.

When we were sad, we cried rivers of tears. As children, we did not need to understand how emotions work, how endorphins are released in our bodies, or what is behind everything. We simply knew how we felt in those moments when we experienced those real emotions and continued with the processing of that information by expressing ourselves freely. Our most significant moments occurred at the perfect time every time we formed a memory imprint.

As children, we began our conditioning into adulthood the day we began to read at age 5. That was a day I will never forget. I remember it as clearly as yesterday. It was glorious! I felt empowered and was aware of a new ability. The power to inform me. We are not taught, however, that we learn from all of our 5 Basic Senses. We do practice how to express ourselves through art and music as well as how to play. We also began our de-evolution through the programming of what society deems what your adulthood should be.

Believe only what you see. Do as you are told. Deny all of your other senses. Control your emotions. Be afraid of enjoying things too much. Believe whatever the tell-LIE-vision tells you to think. Stop acting like a child!

Thank God for all that life presents us with. I would change not one second of any moments I have ever experienced. I am who I am precisely because of the understanding that all of my experiences were necessary for the formation of my Consciousness. All of the experiences stored as memories are useful in learning more about me or sharing what I am learning with others.

I am re-remembering how to feel everything once again. I remain humble in my re-discOVERy of that which I already kNEW as I recOVER my lost inner child. Each layer of truth that is uncOVERed is a R(EVOL)UTION of (EVOL)UTION.

DISSOLVE,
RESOLVE,
(EVOL)VE,
LOVE

CHAPTER TWO

JUST BEING

1. CREATIVE AWARENESS

There is an infinite array of ways to perceive Reality. Even within each of the 8 billion human perceptions, each Being may alter their beliefs to reform how they feel about anything worthy of contemplation. With each conversation about any given topic of discussion, we have an opportunity to receive potentially useful information that we very likely have not yet considered.

Depending on your willingness to learn new points of view, you will go into conversations with varying degrees of receptiveness based on how open-minded you are. If your willingness to become more aware of something is minimal, chances are you will not be very open-minded. If your beliefs are very strongly held, you will not likely hear the message. There are times when another may use just the right word phrasing and tone of voice that elicits an emotional response in you. If you view your emotions as spiritual guides or messaging agents, you will likely pay closer attention to what is occurring.

When we are creative in every way possible, we become aware that the more information we have access to, the more we can learn. The more we learn, the more knowledge we possess. If this knowledge generates joyous feelings, and we are truly grateful for how we feel, we become compelled to share what we learn with others freely. Sometimes we are best suited to teach by simply living by expressing ourselves. If we enjoy nature and how peaceful we feel while basking in the Sun, our emotions radiate from our bodies and we have those great sighs of relief. We exhale carbon dioxide with this expression of satisfaction. Any plants in our vicinity get a nice dose of the food they require to live.

As we become aware of our Consciousness and conscious of our

Awareness, we reach a point of Realized Revelation in which we become able to recognize that all quanta of Energy are useful in illuminating anything that is consciously becoming more aware. In other words...every single experience that occurs to anything conscious of the stimuli becomes more illuminated. The only difference between everything is the degree of illumination and the rate of change that occurs, and the frequency that is felt.

The Law of One describes how all beings are related Spiritually. Quantum Mechanics describes how all things are connected physically. Science is spiritual, a psychology of religion, and a philosophy of faith. Old thought forms are becoming new beliefs. Previously held beliefs are changing into new feelings of Awareness. Indescribable feelings fold back into waves of emotional cleansing agents washing away any recurring toxicity and dissonance. The resolving nature of Sound transforms all Energy into pure Love.

There are no limits to what you can know. To know more about anything, you can discover new aspects about that which you are better understanding by asking questions. If you wish to better understand another Human Being, ask them questions with the pure intention of getting to truly know them. If you wish to know how a process works, ask the why questions and discover its purpose. Once you believe you understand its purpose, you are in a position to reverse-engineer the answers to the how what, and where questions. You will become as aware of whatever you wish by paying attention to however you feel along the quest for knowledge.

Instead of viewing Earth as a training facility or prison, think about Earth as The Ultimate Playground. We have all been excused to go to recess. We have a surprise waiting for us, as the Treasure Hunt begins. Each bit of data, piece of information, and quantum of Energy is a clue. Each clue we collect serves one primary function...to illuminate our Consciousness. Every newly absorbed illumination spins our Oscillating Rate of Frequency faster. As we become more Illuminated, our power grows and calls out to Awareness, which response lovingly with Waves of Sound. Becoming Sound is The Way. The path is lit and we can stay on the path or take detours on our way back home. Life is gifted to us so that we rediscover that the Treasure is the journey.

2. DEGREES OF BEING

All humans exist at various degrees of being. Each of the almost 8 billion different Human Consciousnesses are oscillating at different rates of frequencies and fluctuates those rates faster and slower depending on how they perceive what is occurring in their experience. To use terms such as "higher" or "awake" denotes a "better than" mentality. No being is vibrating at a higher level and all are equal to The One. Even the Other being, Zero, is infinitely more than nothing. All beings are awake and do not need to be awakened. Each will increase its Oscillating Rate of Conscious Frequency when they are ready. All things oscillate at different rates of frequency and nothing is better than anything else. All things exist for a reason and serve a specific function.

As our rate of frequency increases, so does our level of power. This power comes in the form of clarity. Our faster rates of Consciousness perceive more of what is occurring for our benefit, as opposed to what we think is happening to us. The more clear our inner vision, the faster the dissonance resolves. Instead of being confused, we become more peaceful. Any painful experience that occurs to us can disrupt our sense of well-being. If we are patient, the dust will settle and we become clear of vision again. When we choose to remain confused or angry and try to see the light before our field of vision is clear, we are trying to make sense of something without allowing ourselves to receive all of the information. We are only seeing a portion of the story and not viewing the whole picture.

With faster rates of Consciousness comes the expansion of Awareness. If our Consciousness is Who we are, our Awareness is What we are. What we are is Why we are here, for everything we perceive is based on How we feel about it. If we feel peaceful, we are naturally inclined to appreciate that occurrence. If we feel joyful, we enjoy that experience. If we are afraid of something, we tend to resist that occurrence from happening, but get angry when the anxious feelings persist. If we pay attention to those disturbing thoughts that pop into our minds and irritating types of emotions and learn something new about ourselves, we become more aware. We don't have to like this part of the process, but we can at least respect it. As we learn that these types of experiences are very informative, we begin to appreciate these trials. With these tougher and more painful experiences, we become more aware if we accept the information as truthful.

We naturally rejoice when we connect with those who resonate with us consciously. This resonance is felt through vibrations that are Sound. There is a dual meaning in Being Sound. To be Sound is to be peaceful. To be the Sound is to consciously become those Sound frequencies. To become more aware is to allow ourselves to feel Sound. When we resonate with another Being, we become reconnected with each other. We become One with one another. Our frequencies harmonize with others when they are oscillating at a similar rate.

No two things oscillate at the same frequency, for every quantum of Energy that has occurred after the first piece of existent material happened began to exist after that first peace is felt. All other subsequent particles that come into existence cannot occupy the same point in Space. Even if they come into existence at the same moment in Time, due to the convergence of the Space-Time Continuum, there is a perception of partial separation in the frequency. This perception is the illusion of contrast in motion.

The illusion of Reality is meant to gain our attention so that we become more aware of our Consciousness being able to absorb information from more of our senses. We are conditioned to believe only what we see and hear. When we keep an open mind and learn how to access more of the available information that is offered within each occurrence, we become more consciously aware as our Consciousness oscillates at faster rates. Just like we expanded our technology to be able to measure the full spectrum of Electromagnetic Energy, we can tap into our 3 Spiritual Senses (Space, Motion, and Time) while harnessing the 5 Basic Senses. When we use more than our Sense of Sight and Sound, we feel more of a complete vision of the information.

All humans have opportunities to develop these abilities. The only aspect of our being that is required to improve these skills is an active Imagination. A beautiful way to assess the level of your Awareness is how peaceful you feel. Remember...you need not assess the feelings, beliefs, or actions of others because you are responsible for only your Consciousness. You will catch yourself being judgmental when you become irritated, frustrated, angry, or fearful by the actions or words of others. Sometimes we are confused by an occurrence in our Reality. All of these other than peaceful feelings that occur to us happen for a reason. We are given friendly reminders that we are about to become more aware.

Being aware of our feelings has nothing to do with intelligence. I know Human Beings that have Trisomy 21 who are profoundly peaceful, while others who have genius IQs are quite miserable. I contend that any Being who is peaceful, happy, or joyful is oscillating at faster rates of Consciousness. They may not necessarily be able to describe in words just how much they are enjoying life, but express their gratitude by simply laughing and smiling. Any Being who is peaceful will share that Energy freely. Some will give back to the Universe by expressing themselves artistically while others are just happy as they go about their daily lives. Others are very happy to share what they are learning.

3. THE HUMAN FACTOR

What makes us human?

All living organisms share the Four Fundamental Elements of

Hydrogen, Oxygen, Nitrogen, and Carbon. All living organisms share the ability to store genetic information in the DNA and RNA molecules. The genetic difference between *Pan troglodyte* (Chimpanzee) and *Homo sapiens* (Human) is approximately .1%.

Having Consciousness is part of what makes us human, but is only one of many aspects that make us who we are. Various degrees of being conscious exist in everything from subatomic quanta of Energy to Human Beings. Intelligence is only one aspect of what constitutes our brain's ability to process information.

Our Consciousness allows humans to perform many tasks, including communication. We understand that all animals possess this gift, however, so this ability does not set us apart from other animals. There are two aspects of communication that seem to pertain only to humans. The act of written language and the expression of art. I have seen a video in which an Elephant painted its family, but would not have likely done this of its own volition. There are examples in which great apes can use sign language, but cannot form words. The ability to communicate verbally and express our language in written texts and phrases to describe an experience or instruct a reader to take specific steps is uniquely human.

I feel that the one ability that humans are blessed with is Awareness of the gift of Free Will. If we believe that anything is possible, we become aware of how to consciously use our imaginations to create our Reality in the way that we wish to experience it. When we allow ourselves to expand our Awareness by absorbing sufficient amounts of data, without the resistors of fear, we have the Revelation that our feelings are our most efficient and effective source of information.

Having these levels of Awareness is humbling because with great power comes great responsibility. Those who remain thinking that they know what is best for others are not yet aware of what is best for themselves. They may very likely believe that their purpose is to tell others how to think, what to believe, and why they should feel ashamed to believe what they will if it conflicts with what they think. All of these ways of thinking are not only understandable but are quite rational as well.

As a human's Awareness expands, so does their imagination. With a sparking imagination comes more creativity. I feel the Belief System is that part of our perception that allows us to use our imagination freely. We not only imagine creative ways to solve problems, but we also create imaginative ways to perceive our experiences. Problems become puzzles and our quests for knowledge become treasure hunts. Troubling questions become riddles that we realize already have answers. Issues become equations that have built-in solutions. We can ask the Why questions first and reverse-engineer the How, What, and When portions of the formula.

We consciously seek more information as we realize that Knowledge is power. We have revelations that Wisdom is peaceful and gives our lives deeper meaning. When we share what we learn about expanding our Awareness or live by example by simply loving one another, we truly shine and become what we were designed to be...Human Beings.

4. BELIEVING IN LOVE

Our Belief System is the key to our Free Will. If we do not believe that anything is possible, we will be unable to understand why there is suffering in the world and we will misunderstand why we are here on Earth. I feel God's presence and know it is pure Love that is occurring to me. This level of awareness is available to all who believe. The price of admission to the ultimate show costs nothing. All that we need to do, to spend our Time, is pay attention to how we feel currently. How we choose to perceive what is happening matters only to the degree of Awareness we wish ourselves to feel.

Love is nothing to be seen with our eyes. Love cannot be detected with modern technology. We are, however, genetically engineered to specifically feel Love. Hard-core scientists can deny the existence of anything that cannot be observed if they rely on measurable data to be able to prove the existence of whatever they are trying to understand. If that which they are attempting to better know is Spiritual, they will determine their lack of Awareness through their measurements, laws, and theories.

Take the topic of Dark Matter...science has determined that our Universe is composed of 15% observable material called Physical Reality. The remaining known Universe 85% is suspected to be Dark Matter. Physicists admit that they know what Dark Matter is not, but cannot fully grasp what Dark Matter is because it emits no electromagnetic radiation. To admit that if something is not of this Physical Realm and that it might be Spiritual would mean that they believe in something that cannot be proven through observational data. All science is based on measurable evidence that can be proven to exist through experiments that have results that are predetermined to occur 100% of the time. Predictable results seem to satisfy the Collective Consciousness and are accepted as scientific fact.

The funniest thing about proving that Dark Matter exists is predetermined to fail simply because they are searching for a particle that is invisible as it emits no observable EM radiation. Science has set up an unsolvable paradox. As long as the rules for proving anything can be determined by relying on observable data as the evidence that is required to make that theory a fact, the equation will remain unsolved if part of the equation possesses unobservable data. In other words...have fun chasing a ghost you are not meant to see. This does not mean that Dark Matter is an impossibility. My only real issue with Dark Matter is regarding the name science has placed on it.

I know Love exists based on how I feel being loved. Each human has a different perception of what Love is. Some think Love is painful, while others believe Love conquers all. I feel that Love Is The Absolute Truth. To better understand anything, one must only allow themselves to become more aware of what is occurring with that thing. To become more aware of anything, we obtain more information about that which we wish to know better. Therefore, Energy becomes the information and the source is the informant.

If we believe in God in a way that makes sense, we can better know God and how God works. We can choose to perceive God as Pure Frequency, Consciousness, Divine Energy, or as non-existent nothingness.

If all that we do is appreciate what we have, it matters not what you call the One. I feel that regardless of what we perceive, the Creator loves all of the creation perfectly. To love everything, everyone, and every being with pure Love is to do so without condition. There are no expectations that God has for us. The only requirement to survive for three minutes of life is to take one breath. To survive three days, we need only to drink eight glasses of water. To survive three weeks, we are required to a certain amount of calories per pound of body weight. Everything else is determined by the choices we make. All of our experiences are provided for us to be what we are meant to become...Human Beings.

If we find a way to do the toughest thing of all and love ourselves unconditionally, we begin to understand why we are here on Earth. When we have a purpose in our lives, we have reason to live. Our Will to proceed with the journey is strengthened. To choose to continue to process the information that comes in the form of experiences is evidence of Free Will. To have the Revelation that we must exist for not just any reason, but a divinely inspired one, we realize that God truly loves us. As we become more aware of the Absolute Truth that God is all and all is Love, we very naturally choose to love one another.

If you choose to believe in yourself long enough to experience a variety of occurrences, you will better know others. If you understand why others do what they do, you will be able to forgive them. Every interaction is an opportunity to become more aware of others. We are always learning.

5. MIND CONTROL

When another discourages you from believing in anything that you currently understand, they are imposing on your Free Will. They are free to express themselves however they will as per our Free Will Mandate, however, they are also subject to the causality of Karma as all other humans are.

We are all free to choose to perceive and believe however we wish. We are allowed to protect our Spirit along the journey of self-discovery. Instead of trying to understand the intentions of others to determine if they are lying to us, we can gauge our fuel level. If we experience an interaction that includes another who is deceitful or they are passing along information that is misleading because it is fed to them from an agent of deceit, we will feel our Spirit begin to leave our bodies. Although some thoughts of discernment may cross our minds, we are allowed to o be kind to ourselves and turn any disturbing thoughts into peaceful images. When we feel other than Peaceful, we can love the other being and do whatever comes naturally. As we become more aware of why we are here on Earth, we may find ourselves detaching ourselves from that interaction. To endure any suffering, anger, hostility, or hate is only punishing ourselves. Remember...who is in control of *your* mind? YOU ARE!

The easiest way to manipulate another's Consciousness is to implement mind control tactics. Everything comes down to fear. There are degrees of fear ranging from thinking that you need something unnecessary to the terror of feeling alone in the Universe. There is a huge range of beliefs that we call doubts. Non-belief or disbelief are misleading concepts as there are only degrees of belief in anything that you are conceiving. Our ability to doubt, is a gift, though. It is fun to temporarily doubt things. If we are good at thinking thoughts of doubt while manifesting through our feelings of what we truly wish to occur, we amuse ourselves and act surprised when our dreams become our Reality.

If we let doubts turn into anxiety, and fear, we still have a choice. We either remain to experience those frequencies or tune into a new radio station. If we have already learned how certain experiences will feel, and the processing of that type of Energy is painful, we may choose to bypass that off-ramp. If we remain curious and choose to experience whatever is occurring to us, we will, even if we appear to be destroying ourselves. Another who observes our state of being may try to intercede, but until we wish to change, no one can change our mind. We remain in control of our thoughts. If we remain unwilling to change, mind control is effective in holding us in a state of fear, but that is because we invited outside forces into our reality. The most effective mind-controlling agent in Human History is the television.

We are fed pre-programmed streams of data. We happily watch the commercials "suggesting" their products and have become addicted to cable news that tells us what we should fear. All of the programs possess partially true information, so it is somewhat useful. As with all things...we can gauge our feelings and discern between useful data and that which we can discard.

"Adapt what is useful, reject what is useless, and add what is specifically your own." -Bruce Lee

As we become more aware of just how powerful we are, we are wise to remain humble. If we choose the path of darkness, we know deep down that we will not escape Karma. If we choose the Way of the One, we will naturally know what we should do at any given moment. We understand how our actions instantly affect others. We become responsible beings because we know how to inspire others. We are intelligent enough to know how to manipulate others, but we are also wise enough to choose what will feel best for all who are in our circle of influence.

Beware of your own words, as they are real incantations. We have all experienced the true power of the spoken word. Speaking with passion is spellcasting. You have the power to lift another by expressing inspirational combinations and phrasings of words. You can also destroy another by expelling hate-filled and toxic venom that will drain their Spirit. All religions, cults, and secret societies engage in ceremonial rituals that incorporate spells that are referred to as prayers, chants, or incantations. Sometimes, members of these groups lift their Spirits with song and you feel it when this experience occurs.

When you tell another what to think, what they can believe, or how they should feel about anything, you are engaging in mind control. You are imposing your will onto theirs. When you encourage others to feel free to express how they feel, you will be an inspirational influence. We show the deepest levels of compassion by simply sharing what we have learned about how to find peacefulness not despite our experiences, but because of the experiences that occur to us. When we share wisdom without expectations of reward, the Love is felt by both the teacher and the student. I feel that the teacher becomes the student upon the reception of the expansion of Awareness.

6. BECOMING, BEING, BE

Every *Homo sapiens* has the opportunity to become a Human Being. To deny who you are becoming, or what you are being, is to remain at a level of awareness that will be determined by your Consciousness preventing you from knowing what you can be.

To think about something is the beginning of a better understanding. Contemplation is the foundation of using your mind to know anything. Through our thought process, we formulate our ideas into potential outcomes. Our ability to use our Imagination is how we begin to make sense of our Vision. Our logic, rationale, and reasoning are part of our left brain hemisphere, and our intuition, creativity, and holistic approach are part of our right brain hemisphere. When we use both of these parts of our brain in conjunction, we increase our capacity to transform Energy into manifestations of Reality. The start of anything that comes into existence is a Thought Form. Everything is becoming something other.

The only barrier to the further enhancement of our thinking processes is fear. Frank Herbert's book *Dune* comes to mind.

"I must not fear.
Fear is the mind-killer.
Fear is the little-death that brings total obliteration.
I will face my fear.
I will permit it to pass over me and through me.
And when it has gone past I will turn the inner eye to see its path.
Where the fear has gone there will be nothing. Only I will remain."

-Paul Atreides

Thoughts are things. The only thing that holds a thought form in place is a belief. All beliefs are initiated from an understanding of that which is being assessed. Our ability to learn is an allowance of information reception. Without the manifestation of our physical body, we do not have a brain to use as a processing center. Think of the brain as our computer hard drive and our nervous system as the motherboard. If corrupted data is introduced into your hard drive, a virus can occur. Data can be lost and rendered irretrievable. Fear is the actual virus. This does not mean viruses do not serve a vital function. They remind us that our information is sacred. When our computers have a virus, we fear that we will lose our data. In some cases, our computers can be rendered entirely useless. If our computers are hacked, we fear that our information will be used to drain our bank accounts or utilized to obtain financial gain under pretenses.

In the Physical Realm, our bodies are susceptible to viruses being introduced into our systems. We have been conditioned to think that we have no way in which to combat these viruses. This level of belief is fueled by fear. The fear is intense enough that many accept the cure in the form of vaccinations. This level of belief is understandable and even rational to a certain degree. If our bodies no longer function in a manner that allows us to proceed with our Prime Directive, which is to be Transceivers, we will no longer exist in the form of a Human Being. The best part of understanding what our actual purpose for being is we are not required to worry about when we have completed our mission. Our expiration date is predetermined. Our perception of the whole process is always in play. Our Consciousness never dies. Our bodies also never die, as we have expressed in The First Law of Thermodynamics. Nothing ever actually dies; it only transforms from one state of being to another, and another, and another until entropy is reached. This state of being is The Other, which gives rise to a new one and another once again.

Our physical bodies are manifestations of our Physical State of Being. Energy is information. For the information to be transformed into knowledge in the form of memory imprints, we experience an occurrence in the Physical Realm. The Energy in the Electro-magnetic Spectrum is illuminating our molecules and cells, causing a series of chemical reactions that involve our endocrine system. The release of the endorphins is how our physical body "knows" when it's time to receive the love message, which includes loving thought forms and emotions. Our physical body is simply a transceiver receiving light, transforming and storing it until we express our feelings so that others may better understand us. This transformational process is how we go from Becoming basic *Homo sapiens* to Human Beings.

Our Emotional Body is where the magic happens. It is our emotional experiences that make our lives REAL. Without our emotions, we use our emotions to REALize what is occurring in our REALity. If we REAct to stimuli, we feel REAl pain. ARE you listening to your emotions or do you ignore them?

Mental=WHO we are becoming
Physical=WHAT we are being
Emotional=HOW we be

I finally understand what it means to reach *Enlightenment.* I have often contemplated the idea and acknowledge that Enlightenment is not a destination, but a journey. Our Journey of Being Human has always been the processing of Energy. There are levels of Awareness as well as degrees of Consciousness.

To become more conscious of our Mental, Physical, and Emotional States of Being is necessary to become more aware of our Consciousness. Being conscious of our Awareness and how we FEEL, is when we are aware of how to use feelings to expand our Awareness. This transformation from a Human Becoming into a Human Being is truly miraculous. This level of awareness is being informed to the point of illumination. There is an Alpha point that occurs in which we fully REAlize our REAson for being here on Earth. There is a large degree of data that is accepted as Truth that further processes the data to this point of knowing. That Realization is revealed at the perfect moment in Time. That moment is felt so deeply, it is re-FELT to us as a Revelation. The subsequent chapters from that Alpha point Betas in which we store those chapters as memories.

The Omega point of our history is fully known by The One for Human History is His-Story and Her-Story, which is a My-Story and an Our-Story.

If you know your Omega point, share how you came to know it. During the retelling of your story, know the only thing that you currently know, which is how you feel. Express yourself however you wish and remain open-minded, maintain a loving heart, and feel a free Spirit.

ENJOY THE SHOW
FEEL THE RIDE
APPRECIATE IT ALL
JUST BE

7. INFINITY TRINITY

SPACE/TIME/MOTION

To better understand what Infinity is, let us begin with the meaning of the universal ∞ symbol. There are two fundamental elements of existence...Space & Time. This Where and When is the foundation of any occurrence.

To have anything, we need a place for that thing to occur. This *Where* is called Space. Everything begins at its point of origin. This position is known as a Zero Point. Everything that has ever existed has not only a point of origin, but everything shares that same source. This irrefutable truth can be denied if you choose to only believe what you see.

The one thing Everything requires to become an existent occurrence is Time. My ever-growing understanding of Time began with my definition, which came to my Consciousness as a teenager. My dad asked me what my definition was. I answered...Time is the interval between two occurrences. From any point in Space, the change of motion, either in frequency or direction, requires a measurement of Time we call duration. This period is a vector of change. This vector is the interval between two occurrences points A&B (Alpha and Beta). Time is *When* something occurs.

Both Space and Time are Eternally Uniform and emerge as a unified two-dimensional shape we recognize as ∞. Space is immeasurable in size and can be defined as 0. Time can be subdivided linearly to express the duration of a sequence of two or more occurrences. Time in its pure form has an unlimited amount of duration and can be expressed as 0. Both Space and Time are infinite, and when combined, create a two-dimensional Infinity Loop we know ∞.

$$0 \times 0 \approx \infty$$

On a traditional two-dimensional XY graph, if x=Space, and y=Time, then we can view z=Motion. The x-axis becomes left/right and the y-axis becomes up/down. If we spin this graph on its x-axis, the ∞ becomes a toroidal shape much like that of a donut because of the motion. When we can imagine anything in three dimensions at once, we can envision it taking form in our reality.

SPACE-TIME

↘↗

MOTION

So our two-dimensional ∞ symbol becomes a three-dimensional shape that can cause the Fourth Dimension of Form to occur. All three aspects of Infinity have no limitations. Space is immeasurable. Time exists anywhere it causes friction such that an occurrence may appear. Motion can occur in any sequence of events that are observed or felt. The one action that everything that comes into existence shares is that of motion. Everything moves. Even the perfect stillness of Nothingness is temporary.

Our 5 Basic Senses of sight, Sound, Smell, Taste, and Touch all have one thing in common. They all detect different times of Motion. We see visible light from the Electromagnetic Spectrum. Light is the motion of photons. We hear sounds that are felt as a moving wave of air molecules. We smell odorant molecules that must move through our olfactory system. Our sense of taste works similarly as our taste buds sense molecules that cause chemical reactions to occur. All chemical reactions are changes in the motion of elements and molecules. When we touch something, we perceive that point of contact as solid matter, but our skin cells don't touch anything. Instead, our electrons interact with those of the material we are touching. Things in motion detect the motion of other things.

Our 3 Spiritual Senses are felt during our state of being a human on Earth and remain intact after we traverse fully into the Spiritual Realm. We can become aware of our Sense of Space (proprioception), Motion (felt through gravity and balance), and Time. As we become better acquainted with these senses, we become more consciously aware of how to use the information received through these senses to become more knowledgeable about how the Universe operates.

Everything goes back to the One Fundamental Truth...

Anything Is Possible

When we remain Faithful, we maintain peaceful frequencies while becoming more aware during our journey. Our courage, strength, and perseverance are tested, especially when we endure pain, confusion, and obstacles. This entire life experience is designed to test our Will. When we believe that Anything Is Possible, we realize that there is no way to ever truly waste our time, as there is an infinite supply of it.

We feel free to take our time and pay attention to the details so that we may re-remember how to appreciate everything. When we have the Revelation of how to efficiently utilize our Consciousness during our human experience to manifest any possible outcome, we expand our Awareness to points in which we are left in states of sheer awe.

KNOW NOTHING
BECOME AWARE OF
WHAT INFINITY IS

8. NOTHING...MORE TO DISCUSS

I used to believe anything is possible and nothing is impossible. It is perfectly understandable and even reasonable to believe that Nothingness cannot exist.

I feel Space and see things in Space but cannot observe Space, for it emits no EM radiation. For anything to exist, it requires two elements...a where and a when...hence the Space-Time Continuum. Upon anything coming into existence, it would become observable to other things that can view that Energy or would not be recognizable as an existent thing. Upon its emergence into existence, it would occupy a point in Space and have a duration of Time.

If something did not exist, would we be able to contemplate its existence?

All of our Reality is based on the premise that Anything Is Possible, so even Nothingness can exist, or we would be incapable of thinking about it. The only thing that would be left to do is determine a way to manifest that thing into one's Reality. We will things into existence either in the Physical or Spiritual Realm.

I believe that the absence of all EM Radiation can exist but is necessary for only a partial fraction of a picosecond, which allows for a collapse of all energy back into the Absolute Singularity of the 1 only to become the No One (None) of pure 0.

From that point in Space-Time, another 1 re-emerges, and another, and so on.

So...maybe Nothingness possesses a position in Space for a duration of Time. This Nothingness might seem like an Eternity to the one that this occurs as there is nothing to see or feel. There would be no way to measure Time, as there would be no observable EM Radiation through which an already existent thing could have in contrast. Space and Time become irrelevant to the Universe that created that opportunity for that No-Thing to occur.

The next time you believe that something cannot exist, but you are talking about that non-existent thing or even thinking about it, permit yourself to think that anything is possible. Begin with this thought and give it time to become an idea. Over some time, with the allowance of feeling information through all of your senses, that idea will form into a belief. Beliefs are formed through our deeper understanding of that which we are learning. All beliefs can grow into formulated feelings that maintain the frequencies that bring those images into a real state of existence that we call Reality.

Since I believe anything is possible, I can take a concept such as Nothing and realize that it is Something, even if it does not exist in physical form. This thought experiment reconnects back to the notion of Dark Matter, which emits no electromagnetic radiation. We can imagine its existence but have determined its fate through what it has been called. Whenever we accept that everything has a Spiritual Essence, we allow ourselves to believe in that which is not observed and is irrational because it is immeasurable. Therefore, the nothingness of Nothing is something after all. Anything that we can conceive of possesses the SPIRIt or we would not have been InSPIRed to think about it.

KNOW NOTHING

9. FEELING EVERYTHING

I feel everything so I can better understand anything. By maintaining one core belief—*ANYTHING IS POSSIBLE*—I am capable of using all information to create whatever I wish. My Reality is becoming more peaceful than I have previously remembered imagining.

Anything measurable is only one of an infinite array of possible aspects of any given thing which we can try to better understand. Electro-magnetic Radiation emits observable Energy. All Energy is information. The information does one thing for everything else it interacts with...it illuminates everything that allows for that energy to be absorbed. This free flow of Energy causes the effect of transformation. $E=mc^2$ verifies the relationship between Energy and Matter and that transfOrMaTION is generated through MOTION.

That which grabs our attention faster than anything is pain. We can feel pain in each of our Three States of Being (Physical, Mental, and Emotional). It's only when we ignore the pain that we deny ourselves access to valuable information. The Universe has a system in place that provides a built-in reminder of just how vital the information is, that is occurring to us during that moment. For example, touch a hot stove...OUCH! What happened? Your skin tissue has cells that already know that the temperature is too hot and will break down the structure of the cells and cause permanent damage if the correct reaction does not occur. The intensity of the pain is equivalent to the level of awareness one must reach to sustain certain peaceful frequencies. The degree and number of calculations that are required to make your muscles contract and pull away in a fraction of a second, including specific amounts of force, angles of motion, and speed of those movements, is mind-boggling. It is a good thing we do need to solve all of those calculations before performing those actions.

The Reality of our Universe is that Friction is necessary to feel anything through Time and Space. When we do not feel all aspects of an occurrence, we feel degrees of pain commensurate with the level of Awareness. As our Awareness expands, we become more accepting of how much information we choose to allow to be absorbed by our bodies.

That which is immeasurable becomes Spiritual. We become more familiar with anything by experiencing that occurrence utilizing as many senses as possible. We cannot observe that which is immeasurable, but we can experience that occurrence through our feelings. To deny the existence of anything that cannot be observed is to remain unaware of that Spiritual information.

1=phySICALReALITY
0=SpIRituALaCtuALITY

If $E=mc^2$, and as per The First Law of Thermodynamics, the X factor of the creation of an existent thing in our physical reality becomes apparent. Both sides of the Electro-magnetic Spectrum would have to somehow be connected. There would have to be some sort of Energy that exists before AM Radio Waves and something after Gamma Rays. The X, however, is immeasurable because it is unobservable.

Electro-magnetic Radiation emits observable energy.

Dark Matter is believed to compose 85% of our Universe but cannot be seen. It is suspected that gravitational lensing might be evidence of Dark Matter's existence. If Dark Matter emits zero electromagnetic radiation, it has zero mass. Without mass, there is nothing to cause gravitational lensing to occur. Another candidate then presents itself. It seems possible that supermassive black holes are causing the lensing to occur.

Just because something cannot be observed does not mean it does exist on any level of Consciousness.

Nothing matters because Everything matters or it would not occur. Some things exist and cannot be observed but are felt.

Sound, for example...cannot be "seen," but you can observe the effects of sound in the form of waves. We can measure sound frequencies through the medium of air by observing the measurements of these frequencies of the pitch. The Sound Waves themselves are invisible as they possess no Electro-magnetic Radiation. We are only seeing various mediums oscillate because of the Sound Waves moving that material. You can hear sounds both in the Physical Realm as well as the Spiritual Realm of your mind. Music moves us, even when we have that song stuck in our heads, because of how it makes us feel.

Our Senses of Sight, Smell, Taste, and Touch are all measurable because of how Energy is transmitted, transferred, and transforms as it is being processed. Pieces of matter can be detected on a quantum level because of our technology. The naked eye can only detect .0035% of all of the Electromagnetic Spectrum. Our bodies, however, can feel Energy beyond what can be seen.

$$X=0$$
$$Y=1$$

The perfect balance of Yin/Yang addresses that which many misunderstand as the purpose of pain, misery, and suffering. When we allow ourselves to feel everything, we learn what we are designed to learn at faster rates of Consciousness and expand our Awareness into deeper levels of inner Space.

Consciousness goes from being Who we are to When we are and Awareness goes from How we feel to Where we are.

$$\text{Consciousness}=(T)\text{ime}$$
$$\text{Awareness}=(S)\text{pace}$$

Both Time and Space are infinite, immeasurable, unobservable, and necessary components in the creation of anything in our Physical Reality. The more you feel, the more Energy will be transformed. All information becomes knowledge upon the acceptance of this transaction. With the absorption of every piece of illumination comes an increased rate of conscious frequency. For every single bit of data (photon) that occurs, we have one Planck length of time that moves. The Planck constant describes how much the energy of a photon increases when its electromagnetic frequency increases by 1 SI unit. This rate increase is mind-bogglingly small, but so are photons. 1.8×10^{20} photons per second are generated by a 60-watt light bulb. Think of how much heat is generated by a 60-watt light bulb over any period and you begin to understand the relationship between Energy and how much power is necessary to form matter.

I admit that the size of these numbers is very difficult to imagine, but sometimes learning requires us to stretch our minds and bend time to process the information. I trust the math of the scientists who formulated these concepts into verifiable equations. I graciously ask that while you better understand anything, you simply acknowledge that much of what you feel may be partially understood if at all. All feelings, however, possess useful information for anyone willing to become more aware.

PART THREE

ENERGY IN MOTION

CHAPTER ONE

E-MOTIONS

1. WHAT ARE EMOTIONS?

Or rather, e-motions?

Emotions are an energetic means of passing along information. While existing in human form, we gather information through our Earthly Senses. We are inundated with a vast array of experiences that allow various aspects of our Consciousness to receive data, and process it.

What causes us to think? Is it not our feelings? Which form of our feelings most easily gains our attention? I contend that our most powerful feelings are those of Emotion. Even before we are consciously aware of what is occurring to us as infants, we experience feelings such as hunger, anxiety, temperature variants, loneliness, and expressions of love. All of these experiences cause us to feel emotions such as anger, sadness, and happiness. An emotion is a combination of a thought form and a feeling.

Emotions are felt, and yet feelings encompass so much more than emotions. This assessment of emotions does not diminish their effectiveness. I am just proposing that there is much more to the scope of Feelings than just Emotions. Emotions possess the aspect of feelings in that they are being felt, but from a conceptual standpoint, a majority of feelings have no conceptual meaning.

Emotions≈Feelings

For starters...it is impossible to hurt another being's feelings since feelings are spiritual. Spirit cannot be harmed in any manner. One's Spirit can be drained, but that SPIRIt will seek out other bodies that wish to become more illuminated or refilled through being InSPIRed. When someone says that they have hurt emotions, they are feeling emotions that cause pain.

All emotions are powerful means of becoming more informed. Every emotion is telling you a story. You are your author. You have already written your story, but you have to un-remember everything and plant yourself back into the retelling of your own story. Your life is designed for you to not just retell your story, but live it in real-time.

Every story you ever read or see on television or in a theater is providing you with information. The extent of emotional content will gain your attention and allow you to maintain whatever frequency that resonates with you. If a story only has objective data and nothing subjective, the story is informational but lacks emotional content. An engrossing story has a balance of detailed information that is descriptive in a manner that creates vivid imagery as well as strong emotions. The same story when spoken adds even more emotional content. When that story is retold with video, then you add visual imagery that evokes even more emotions. Add a musical score and sound effects, then you incorporate even more emotional content. For this reason, movies and television shows capture our imaginations.

Our strongest emotions are those which tend to cause the more dramatic reactions. Fear, hatred, anger, jealousy, envy, and disgust fall into this category. All of these types of emotions are quite useful tools in recognizing specific lessons. Higher degrees of fear in the terror range will cause our heart to increase its rate, which signals our endocrine system to release adrenaline, which allows us to act out our fight or flight response. In this case, the lesson is simple...our physical well-being is in danger of being severely harmed.

When we feel hatred, we are being taught that there is someone or something that we are misunderstanding. We become confused when we do not understand the purpose of a certain process. That lack of clarity causes us to become annoyed. If we ignore these annoyances, they turn into irritations, frustrations, anger, and eventually, hatred. These mixed emotions are tougher to decipher and our chance of overreaction increases at an alarming rate.

Any other emotions that are other than the peaceful (OTP) category all have lessons to be learned. Anger is felt when we have the notion that we have no control over how we feel. We feel jealousy when we are afraid of losing a partner in a relationship to another being.

We feel envious when our pride is unchecked and we lack a degree of humbleness that keeps us grounded. Disgust is a simple lack of respect for a creature, a being, or a process.

All of these OTP emotions are not to be controlled. When we suppress these emotions, we bury that energy and it builds up in our systems. They will accumulate into toxic levels and affect our physical, mental, and emotional well-being.

If ignored, we may overreact by having an emotional outburst that can be destructive or even deadly. If we are tormented sufficiently mentally, our defense mechanism is to hide and survive. We develop multiple personalities, hear voices, or have very destructive thoughts that can be utterly terrifying. These mental disorders and illnesses lead to various institutions or suicide. Lastly, when we accrue enough toxicity internally, our physical bodies break down and become diseased.

There is an answer to solving all emotionally charged issues. All that we need to do to process the information that is delivered to us is express ourselves. It does not matter how, when, or where; just express yourself at the critical moment in which the pain is too much to bear. Express yourself however you wish. You can express yourself by taking a walk outside. You can let out a primal scream. You can dance, draw, write, paint, sing, play a musical instrument, listen to music, or hug a fellow human being. Each of us is uniquely gifted to be able to freely express ourselves. This is how we use Free Will Whenever, Wherever, and However, We Choose.

The best part about emotions is that there are an array of peaceful ones that cause us to feel indescribably well. Love, joy, hope, compassion, gratitude, honor, respect, and appreciation all help show us how to simply be peaceful, happy, and content.

Do you appreciate how you feel currently? Do you wish to maintain those frequencies? Show your gratitude by expressing yourself by simply sharing that Energy with Everyone you encounter. When you share the Love freely and without hesitation, fear, worry, doubt, expectations, or assumptions of any kind you will feel Peaceful, Joyful, Happy, and Loved. The Universe gives back all Energy you share with others.

LOVE ONE ANOTHER
LOVE YOURSELF
LOVE GOD

2. ABSOLVING SOLUTIONS

I begin all thought experiments, idea creations, or vision manifestations with one premise...

ANYTHING IS POSSIBLE

Beginning the creation, formation, or generation of an idea seems to be processed more efficiently through the maintenance of this one belief. I consider this belief a valid truth. Probability and certainty principles are applied, but always with the underlying foundation of unlimited possibilities. Until this belief is no longer a useful means to facilitate the creative process, I will adhere to this and any belief that allows for my Consciousness to increase its rate of frequency and the Awareness to expand without any limits.

I use all possible data to construct the final image of what I wish to perceive in my Reality. I understand all points of view as being equally valid and a piece of the puzzle that is being solved. I reform my cohesive beliefs without fear of loss or attachment. When I get "stuck" or confused, I transition from logical to intuitive thought and go from accepting knowable data to the allowance of experiencing feelings as the most viable information.

When I feel Peaceful about something, I resolve the riddle by accepting the answer that I have formulated. I allow my belief to be reformed because I have changed my perception through the illumination of new information. I take on all questions with an Open Mind, Compassionate Heart, and Free Spirit. As I resolve any unanswered questions, I feel more Peaceful than before and proceed with simply being.

Instead of viewing anything as a problem, I go into my new adventure with the belief that there is already a solution. If our destiny is preordained, we can simply play our role of service as an Energy Processing Unit(EPU). The entire Creation of Reality has already been conceived and designed to perfectly transform from one state of being to the next one. The transformation of each Human Being is already known to The One, but we perceive our processing from our unique perspective. There are currently 8 billion different Consciousnesses viewing the Universe. Each Human Being is existing, or their Reality would not occur to them.

As you accept the simple truth that there are no problems or even issues, and only solutions, you will view each new experience from the standpoint of simple discovery. To make the journey even more interesting, we can re-remember that we already know what we are supposed to know. Discovery becomes more of a Recovery Mission in which we recollect that viable data. From there, we proceed with the processing of the Energy and the reFORMulATION of inFORMATION.

Take your biggest fear and absolve that. Ask yourself why that which you fear the most is occurring to you. Think of whatever comes into your mind as a possible answer and see how that answer feels. Do that without prejudice and with an open mind. If the answer makes sense, roll with it. Allow your preconceived ideas and previously held beliefs to change and be reformed into new information. You neither wasted your Time or Energy having held onto that previous belief because it got you to where you are currently. Remember...there are no sins, accidents, mistakes, or coincidences. There are only Sines, Signals, Symbols, and Synchronicities.

I AM PROCESSING
LIFE AS I'M DESIGNED

3. transFORMATION of inFORMATION

Energy is only information until it is received and absorbed, at which time it becomes transformational and resolving of any remaining pain.

That storage of dissonant frequencies causes stress on our nervous system. This is why we should not control our emotions but learn how to respond by expressing how we feel. This is the most effective means of releasing that energy through the transformation of that energy.

The only thing to ever reconsider is how you are currently feeling. Upon recognizing painful emotions, love the ones who you think are the cause. Remember...you are in control of your Consciousness. You dictate what comes in and how to perceive it. You allow yourself to hold onto whatever feelings you wish to continue to experience. You either listen to your emotions or ignore them.

You always know how you feel, even if you are not able to describe it in words. When another being is sending mixed signals, it is because they are unclear as to what they wish to communicate. We are often asked by others if there is an issue or how we are feeling. We might say "I don't know," but we know how we are feeling, but trying to make sense of it. We typically remain confused and unsure of what it is we are feeling because we try to use our current level of thinking. Our thoughts don't make sense and will seem nonsensical.

The most effective way to continue the process of transformation is to use the information that has been provided, but to use all of your senses to take hold and do what they do best...move the Energy through your body. We are so addicted to learning by what we see and hear that we often disregard or flat-out ignore our other senses.

We have 5 Basic Senses that I believe we all understand and use. We do tend to be yet able to acknowledge that the Senses of Smell, Taste, and Touch are all quite useful as ways in which to receive information that will allow us to become more aware of our surroundings, and other beings and what they have to offer in terms of Energy.

We also have 3 Spiritual Senses, including Space, Motion, and Time. We can use our Sense of Space to know where to place our limbs while maneuvering through dark places. This is called Proprioception. We can feel our movements through our Sense of Motion. This sense is felt through the effects of Gravity. We maintain our balance through this sense and can estimate our speed on Earth. Time is sensed differently for each being. An hour spent by two different beings in the same room will feel different to each one.

The more of your senses you utilize to experience an occurrence, the more sense it will make. With this influx of information, by keeping an open mind, a compassionate Heart, and a free Spirit, you the more information you will absorb. The more information that is fully processed, the more transformation will occur to your being. This full immersion of Energy brings illumination. The more illuminated you become, the clear you will be. The more lucid you are, the more smoothly your thought process becomes, and the easier your decisions will be made. The levels of peace and joy that come with the learning process expand with the amount of Energy that you process. The reason for these lighter-than-air feelings is due to the transformation of denser EarthBound Emotions to less dense Spiritual Feelings.

Keep in mind that all of your experiences were meant for you or they would not have occurred. Every single moment that has happened shaped your perception of Reality. All inFORMation is transFORMational and will FORM your thoughts into ideas that inspire your beliefs and allow you to feel however you wish.

ALLOW YOUR BODY TO RECHARGE

SHARE WHAT YOU LEARN

ENJOY THE TRANSFORMATION

LOVE ALL

4. EVOLVING RESOLUTIONS

What we think of as problems in life are simply mysteries that already possess solutions. We encounter an experience that makes us feel a certain emotion or combination of emotions. These emotions trigger thoughts, which turn into curiosity. If we wish to become more knowledgeable, we ask the Universe a question or series of questions. If we are still and listen, the answers come in thought forms and feelings that turn into ideas that modify our previously held beliefs or form new beliefs. Through the acceptance of the truth about ourselves, we can resolve the equation into a solution that absolves our Consciousness.

That level of allowance is felt as a strong wave of peacefulness that expands our Awareness. I feel that the process of Awareness expansion is quite simple. As Human Tryings, we think that we have to act a certain way and forget how to simply do things. Even if we become Human Doings, we too often remain believing that we have to do things in a certain way. I strongly feel that we can break through to the other side by becoming Human Beings.

When you are stuck in the Mental Realm, you will become frustrated, confused, angry, and anxious. When you deny these types of emotions by suppressing or ignoring them, you deserve to feel however you do. I understand that this may sound harsh, but if you dig deep and listen to the message, you will see the truth in this information. If you are like I was, you will relate to this behavior, which is akin to Obsessive Compulsive Disorder, if not an indication of possessing OCD. Before you start feeling bad about how you are currently processing inFORMATION, begin your transFORMATION by accepting this aspect of yourself. You are in transition and will be reforming your thought process consciously and in a conscientious manner. The mind is capable of enduring a great deal of stress. By allowing that stress to continue without resolving the issues, your physical and emotional well-being is at risk of becoming unbalanced.

We can become stuck in unresolved physical issues just as easily as mental ones. When we do not respect our bodies, we consume food or beverages that cause damage to our organs at worst or at minimum lower the rate of our vibration. We wonder why we feel lethargic, become obese, or get ill with the disease. We mask the physical pain with opiates and then become addicted to them. At some point, our bodies either break down or shut down. We can choose to listen to our bodies and find solutions to these toxic build-ups before we reach these breaking points.

Oftentimes, we succumb to the conditioning of the notion that we are supposed to control our emotions. By doing this, it is very easy to forget that we have emotions for a reason. The emotions we have are not intended to torment us. We are genetically designed to pay attention to our emotions. When we suppress our emotions, we will endure the same emotions until we have an emotional breakdown and decide that something will have to change. We can always become emotionally rebalanced when we resolve whatever past trauma plagues us.

Have you ever asked yourself why the same type of experiences continue to occur to you? Do you feel like you are stuck in an endless loop of doom? Each resolution absolves you of friction we call pain. Whenever you have an AH-HA moment, you reveal a deeper truth through the allowance of the information to do its thing...illuminate your being. If the pain of whatever is being offered is bearable, chances are you will continue to disregard the experience as an annoyance and let it reappear over and over again. When you reach the point of entropy in which the pain becomes intolerable, you have a mental, physical, or emotional breakdown. That rebuilding of whatever state of being is needing to be redeveloped results in a blissful state of joy and achievement. The level of pain that you allow yourself to suffer has a direct correlation to the level of truth that is available for you to accept. Each resolution brings levels of mental peace, physical joy, and emotional bliss, depending on which state of being was addressed.

Finding useful information in the facilitation of this process of Energetic Transformation is as simple or complicated as you make it. Choosing to believe anything is useful in resolving the mystery that you are unraveling because each thing you believe in is due to your level of understanding about it. Your understanding is based on how you feel about that which you believe. I strongly feel that every belief is partially true, and to better understand it, we discover more truth by breaking through the illusions that hold our attention while we process the information. This process may sound complicated, but it can be summed up in three words: trust your feelings.

Your Reality is based on your perception of what you think is happening versus what is occurring in the Universe. Your level of understanding about anything is whatever you allow yourself to know. You can know the answer to any question you will ever have if you believe that anything is possible. Without this foundational point of better understanding anything, your thoughts will distract you from your feelings, which possess the information that will alter your Belief System. All of this processing of information, transformation, and expression of the Energy occurs between the communication of your Consciousness and the Awareness.

Allow youR emotions to flow freely. Use all of your senses to feel the Energy that is transmitted to you. Accept the information as useful and filter out the most relevant data. This processing and transformation of the Energy allow the absorption of information into every cell of your body. Your cells know what they need to function. Their illumination causes the other metabolic functions to occur and all work towards causing your Consciousness to increase its rate of oscillation. The effect is a deeper expansion of Awareness. You'll know when this happens because of the feelings that will occur.

5. DIVINE TIMING

We often misinterpret the timing of occurrences as being ill-timed. We say things, like "That was bad timing..." or "I was in the wrong place at the wrong time." I feel that nothing that occurs to us is ever ill-timed, bad, wrong, or accidental. All experiences occur exactly when they are supposed to. Experiences can possess degrees of friction from annoyingly irritating to horrifyingly painful.

The good news is that we can break the cycle of recycling the same painful experience over and over again. The moment we have the Revelation that pain is not intended as a type of punishment, we can begin to understand that pain is a form of communication. What is the pain trying to say? Begin with realizing that the level of pain relates directly to the degree of importance that the lesson is teaching. In other words...the more painful the lesson, the more imperative it is that you pay attention to how you feel in the moment that pain is felt as the resolution of the issue will have an equivalent amount of peace.

We need not wait until the pain becomes unbearable. If we better understand the purpose of friction, we can recognize small degrees of friction before it turns into those high degrees of pain. Instead of ignoring the annoyances, we can become more aware of how we feel by paying attention to what we feel at any given moment.

All of our experiences are Divinely Timed. As we learn how to more efficiently process our feelings, we realize the power of our Consciousness to cause our reality to occur. This means that we need not suffer any longer unless we wish to feel the relief of resolving intense amounts of Energy that are presented as high degrees of pain.

If each experience is divinely timed, then the implication of what this means is staggering. I can't help but think about what God's level of knowledge would have to be, for all of these pieces of information to fit so perfectly as they fall into place. It quite simply means that God has these offerings planned out, especially for us. God knows us better than we know ourselves and this includes how we will respond or react to the stimuli that are offered.

As we develop our Consciousness and expand our Awareness, we learn how to go from reacting out of fear to responding out of faith. God knows that until we become fully realized and self-aware, we will react in ways that cause others to experience pain. This entire process of Awareness expansion is directly linked to our Free Will.

All humans can get stuck on the misunderstanding of how God can allow any being to suffer. We can even ask a question such as...

Why would God cause any being to suffer?

The answer becomes clear...

God would never cause any being to suffer. God does not destroy, God creates.

To better understand the process of Energy transformation is to better understand why all things exist in the Universe. All things are created to serve a specific function. All beings exist for a special reason. All things exist to simply be or they would not occur. By simply being, all things are receiving Energy, transforming it, and recycling it by expressing it.

Some beings consciously choose to become more aware of what they are. Those who become fully self-realized accept all aspects of their being, including every single experience that has led them to have enough of a degree of understanding, that they become aware of what they are. This level of knowledge is such that they have enough Faith to persevere while feeling confident that they will fulfill their destiny. Regardless of the specifics of their particular role, they acknowledge that they not only exist for a reason but that their existence is part of the Cosmic Mirror Puzzle. Their Consciousness is perfectly placed in Space and Divinely Timed.

We are all going through the same process as God goes through. This is how God knows what is best for us. This explanation makes perfect sense to me. If it doesn't resonate with you, that is understandable and even reasonable. I am not here to change what you think, why you believe whatever you do, or how you feel about anything. I will express myself, however, I feel as if I am guided to do so. I wish to inspire others to do the same as they process the information from their unique perception and point of view. Spend your time wisely by paying attention to how you are currently feeling. Use all of your senses and become more aware of everything that occurs to you.

PEACEFUL NOW
I AM BEING

6. W.A.V.E.S

I believe the most powerful and efficient waves are those sine waves of Consciousness. We receive Electromagnetic radiation through our senses. The Sense of Sight is the easiest way to recognize and decipher the information. We are attracted to shiny objects. Every day we look up and see the Sun, we are reminded of our Energy Source. Whenever we see a rainbow, we remember the covenant that God will provide life-sustaining water, nutrients for our bodies, and systems that process the Energy that is so freely provided.

All of these transmissions of Energy alter the rate of oscillation of our Consciousness. Biochemical reactions are triggered and endorphins are released, causing us to emote that Energy. It is becoming apparent just how vital our emotions are in modulating our rate of Consciousness.

The more of the senses we employ, the more Energy is received. The more information we transform, the faster our Consciousness oscillates. As the rate of the conscious frequency increases, more power is generated.

I feel that the most effective waves are those of Awareness. I am beginning to view emotions as a Spiritual Force that moves the Wave of Awareness. The more friction that is generated, the more emotional force will be required to move that energy through our bodies. It just dawned on me that each of our three brains is capable of detecting emotional content that comes with the reception of information that is being absorbed in our bodies.

As our Consciousness gains power, the size of the sine wave decreases. We cannot observe the conscious wave of Energy but can make the connection between the behavior of Electromagnetic Radiation as well as Sound Waves. Using our technology, we have been able to measure EM Radiation from AM Radio to Gamma Rays. Before any technology outside of that of harnessing Mechanical Energy, Humans could feel degrees of EM Radiation through our senses but only can measure that Energy from the visible light spectrum. We can currently measure the wavelength and frequency of observable EM Radiation. The more powerful the Energy, the shorter the wavelength and the faster it oscillates. The correlation between the position in Time and Space of the sine wave and its power is evident.

We can see the same inverse relationship between size and efficient power in Sound Waves. I am a musician and have been a sound engineer and understand how much amplitude is necessary to move certain frequencies. We describe faster-moving frequencies as "high" and slower-moving ones as "low," which can be a little confusing regarding the loudness. Even the sound's loudness being described as its volume is misleading because the "volume" of sound correlates to the number of molecules being moved through the air, not the size of the wavelength. I prefer to describe those slower-moving frequencies as bass and faster-moving frequencies as treble. There are subcategories of these, but most of us understand how altering the bass or treble on our stereos affects the sound. Because the faster-moving treble frequencies have smaller wavelengths and less distance between the crest and the trough of each wave, their overall size moves through the air with more ease. This is due to its inherent power. The higher the kinetic energy, the less power in the form of amplitude (amps) is required to move the air toward the listener. A small club, for example, would often not need to mic up anything on a drum kit except for the kick drum, whose primary function is to move bass frequencies through the air. The bass frequencies require more power to have a balanced volume or apparent loudness with the other frequencies.

We can make the same connection between EM Radiation and Consciousness if we view conscious frequencies as having the same penetrating ability with power increases. The more something can penetrate, the easier it can move through various layers of density. For this reason, with faster rates of Oscillating Consciousness, more clarity we have.

With clarity of inner vision comes less confusion. The less confused we are, the less chance of us becoming frustrated, angry, and anxious. In other words...the more peaceful we become.

Along the way of us transceiving, transforming, and transponding Energy, we traverse and transcend through the Universe. With ascension comes more information that becomes useable knowledge that we classify as wisdom. The entire process is a communion between our Consciousness and Awareness. I am becoming more aware of how vital of a role our emotions play in this processing of Energy.

From the instant of reception to the processing and reformation of the thought to its formation of a manifested Reality, emotions are prevalent. The more intense the emotion during any point of the process, the closer attention one should pay. I have been so focused on painful experiences, I have lost sight of the pleasurable ones. Regardless of where the emotion falls on the Pleasure/Pain scale, the level of intensity dictates the relevance in that place in Time and position in Space (Splace).

We are supposed to enjoy the entire experience, including the whole range of emotions. When we experience intense pleasure, if we assume that we deserve to feel that way for any length of time beyond what the feeling is intended for us to experience, we are paying more attention to the mental constructs (thought forms) than emotions. When this occurs, we miss out on the level of awareness that was offered. Time seems to fly when we are having fun. We can immerse ourselves in an experience through the emotional content by simply feeling those emotions by allowing the waves to move us along the way. The more time our attention is spent feeling the whole experience, the less relevant Time becomes. During these Spiritual occurrences, we feel timeless and peaceful.

We can achieve profound expansions of Awareness during extremely painful experiences as long as we pay attention to how we feel.

Instead of ignoring the painful messages, or having an expectation that they will last forever, we can simply absorb the information and use it to learn something new. Regardless of the range of emotions we feel or the degree of pleasure or pain that occurs to us, the most peaceful information exists within the Zero Point of Now.

How ready and willing are you to expand your Awareness?

(W)ILLING
(A)WARENESS
(V)IBRATES
(E)MOTIONS
(S)OUNDLY

7. SPIRITUAL AIKIDO

Aikido is a Japanese martial art that is translated in English to mean "the way of unifying (with) life energy" or "the way of harmonious spirit." A Google translation generated the word "meeting" which makes perfect sense.

I studied Aikido for approximately one year before my daughter was born in 2004. I practiced it again two years ago for several weeks but kept getting nauseous. My Sensei reminded me that I can practice Aikido in the mental and emotional states of being. The title of my piece regarding how I still practice Aikido being called "Spiritual Aikido" may seem redundant, but will make more SENSE when you hear my description. It would be an honor for me to be your SENSEi today.

My understanding of Aikido is that it is very Taoist. The first aspect of any experience that occurs to you is going to be based on your perception. If you view another being as an attacker, you have predetermined that your interaction is going to be one of conflict. When we view any experience as an offering, we are in the best position to be receptive. If the interaction is an offering, then the one with whom we are going to communicate is about to present us with a gift.

If we refer back to the translated definitions of "the way of unifying life energy" or "the way of harmonious spirit," we see the correlation between unification, energy, and Spirit. The most recognizable type of interaction in our Earthly Realm is one of a physical connection. This is due to friction expressing itself as physical pain. The first lesson in pain is formed as a memory imprint because of the intensity of the friction.

Instead of perceiving another being as an attacker, we may view that being as our partner who is offering a gift of Energy. The gift is received as a blessing and upon first contact, a blending of energies occurs. Harmonious resonance begins the composition. We can view this not just as a communication, but as a piece of music with the first chord a perfect 5th called a power chord. This combination of two fundamental notes is the 1st and 5th degrees of a major scale. A major triad is the 1,3,5 of that same major scale.

The next movements in the song are poetically powerful. These dance motions are spiral, elliptical, and smoothly flowing. These waves of Energy transform from different color frequencies into flavors that turn into tasty combinations of Sound. Aikido practiced in the Physical Realm is truly amazing. You incorporate all 8 Senses...the 5 Earthly ones and the 3 Spiritual Senses of Space, Motion, and Time. The beautiful harmonization of Energy results in the resolution of Peacefulness.

Our mental and emotional states of being are always in play, including when we are present in the Physical Realm. We use our thoughts and emotions to assess the information that is provided to us. I believe that Spirit moves instantaneously throughout the Universe and arrives in our Subconscious Mind before any other form of communication. Feeling the Spirit is often described as our Intuition. These feelings trigger thoughts, which cause our emotions to become present. If we accept our thoughts and emotions and use them to process the data without any barriers, we form that information into ideas that change our beliefs. If we are out of balance in any of our Trinity of States of Being, we get stuck. For example...if we become ANGRy during an encounter, the conversation becomes an ARGumeNt. If we allow that AnGER to become RAGE...the ARGumEnt turns into a physical fight.

If we are being Peaceful or becoming Peaceful, we are in a position to assess the information that is offered instead of judging it. When we judge, we are building barriers to the reception of the information freely absorbed into our bodies. Those barriers are fear-based resistors that prevent the entire download from occurring. Misinterpreted thoughts cause us to be confused. That confusion turns into frustration, which makes us anxious. This leads to higher degrees of fear making us angrier still. If left unchecked, that anger turns into destructive rage.

When we are as fearless as possible, we are truly free to explore our Consciousness as we become more aware of just how powerful our Imaginations are. Our power comes from our Life Force Energy which is referred to as Qi, Ātman, Rūh, or Spirit. We are becoming more aware of the Spirit and the Soul, but are recognizing that the Spiritual nature of all aspects of being is real.

8. EVERYTHING SIMPLY IS

In a Universe of uncertainty, we can become aware of one inevitable thing...

All THINGS RETURN TO THE ONE.

Regardless of what we think, say, or do, we all return to the Eternal Now. This When has no end. That Where has forever. The Other is perfectly still and utterly silent.

We can worry, live in fear, cause destruction, and suffer or...we can rejoice and triumph as we re-remember how to simply be. No matter what occurs in your life, you have the gift of Free Will that allows you to choose how to perceive all of your experiences.

Look back on your life and remember any event that caused you much anxiety before it occurred. Did worrying prevent that event from occurring? Was the event even nearly as horrible as you imagined it would be?

Could the entire process have been quite different, depending on your beliefs?

How you answer these questions can alter your perception of the process of learning. Once you recognize that everything is an illusion and your Reality is occurring, then you will recall that you alone are responsible for only one Consciousness...your own.

The best part of the entire Life Occurrence is that you are not alone in the experience. Being responsible for your Consciousness frees you of all other burdens of transmutation. We are not here to fix others, for they are not broken. We are not here to find others, for they are not lost. We are not here to save others, for we are already saved or we would not exist.

The Universe is perfectly ordered and intricately designed. The beauty of all things can be observed if you truly see what you are looking at in the present moment. The purpose of every living organism and particle that exists is felt when you are still and listen.

Use your Conscious Awareness to observe and feel all that is presented to you and then you will know…

BE STILL AND LISTEN
KNOW WHY YOU ARE
HERE ON EARTH

PEACEFUL NOW
I AM
MICHAEL

9. cOmMunicaTION of eMOTION

Our ability to consciously communicate is one of our most valuable gifts. When we use our cOmMunicaTION skills, we are emitting eMOTIONalinfOrMaTION putting our Energy into MOTION. The amount of Enlightenment any human wishes to receive is determined by each Sentient Human Being. Before becoming aware of how to become more illuminated, each human experiences as much information as is necessary to have that proverbial light switch to be flipped to the ONepositiON.

To be turned "ON" is to be inspired to the pOiNt of one's ImaGINatiON to be IGNIted. This ignitION switch being flipped is a SIGNificantrealizatION that results in a huge surge of energy because there is an increase in the rate of oscillating frequency that occurs. The ability to consciously alter our Consciousness and expand our Awareness is a beautiful revelation. Understanding that this level of Awareness has everything to do with our ability to consciously communicate is paramount to our self-realization.

Every emotion that has ever occurred to every human has happened for a reason. Some feel emotions more strongly than others. A recognizable term for such a being is an empath. If one feels little emotions, they are described as being apathetic. We are programmed to believe that we should control our emotions. If you are a woman and you express strong emotions such as rage, it is common to be accused of being hysterical. If you are a man but surrounded by other alpha males, and you show emotions such as deep sorrow, you might be accused of being a crybaby. These are just two examples in which expressions of two emotions, anger and sadness, are highly discouraged in society.

To be conditioned to the point of being brainwashed into believing that we are supposed to suppress our emotions is quite an imposition of our Free Will. To learn how to express our emotions in a manner that transforms that energy into something creative is quite a beautiful experience. As young children, we are taught in preschool about art, playing, singing, and dancing. All of these activities are ways in which we express our emotions. Being creative is therapeutic for all ages and has nothing to do with talent, skill, or intelligence.

Unfortunately, however, we find our society encouraging those we deemed as gifted to pursue those creative art forms. Those children who are not perceived as having skills in art, dance, or music reach an age in which they are encouraged to only do those things for fun in their free time if at all. If a child shows promise in academics, we encourage them to pursue that type of knowledge through the university system. We dismiss the handy or mechanically inclined kids and focus on the academically advanced kids. The kids with below-average intelligence are almost completely ignored or at best thought of in terms of requiring help their entire lives aka needy.

The absolute truth is that all of our kids have so much to offer and serve their purposes exactly as they are designed to do. Everything that we encounter as emotional problems can be traced back to childhood experiences that were traumatic for that being who is trying to be the adult they are supposed to be, instead of the child they were made to be.

As we re-remember what we learned in art class, music lessons, and on the playground, we have our deepest revelations of what it means to be childlike and truly enjoy life. We are genetically designed to laugh, smile, move our bodies, sing, and just play. By consciously using our imaginations, we naturally express ourselves freely and without the inhibitions, society places on us.

All of these expressions of creativity are communications between all beings in that field of influence. So...any who is within line of sight or earshot will see and hear fun activities occurring. Those who need to be inspired will get the message. Anyone who appreciates that simple act of having fun will let you know by communicating with you laughs of joy and smiles of happiness.

When we are not feeling those joyful emotions, we should feel free to express those emotions as well. Our family and friends serve as our energy-processing agents simply by being there to listen and put their arms on our shoulders or be the first to hug us. That transformation of Energy is how we process our emotions through more dense levels to the lighter ones in which we see clearly. Oftentimes, those moments include tears of gratitude for having our loved ones there in our lives willing to physically help with our transformations.

All of these cOmMunicaTIONs are the utilization of eMOTIONalinfOrMaTION to allow for our transfOrMaTION to occur.

CHAPTER TWO

POEMS ARE PEACEFUL

1. ALL THINGS

All of these things are meant to be.
Perception's based on how you See.

The Universe is where you Are.
Floating through Space Around the Star

Of Fire and light from Above
Will make you glow Full Of Love.

When you feel the rage Within
Accept it not as a sin.

However you feel you do deserve,
Just remember who You serve.

AH-MEN

2. THE AWARENESS PRAYER

God, bless me with the Knowledge to increase my rate of Consciousness to become as Powerful as I can be, to always remember to be Aware that Being Peaceful is The Way I remain humble in Being of Service to Others.

As I accept all Truths with an Open Mind, I shall Keep Breathing so that my Compassionate Heart remains beating as long as I am blessed with Life Force so that I may fulfill my Destiny.

I will maintain all Wisdom by being Conscious of my Awareness and abilities to allow all Beings to continue on their journey by encouraging and inspiring them to be True to Themselves no matter what occurs in their Reality.

I promise to remain Faithful as I face all fears and Always Believe in myself as my Awareness Expands with my Free Spirit.

AH-MEN

3. NOW HERE THIS!

Oh, dearest of Spirits,
Now here this!
There's truly Nothing
To the Abyss.

Somewhere, nowhere,
Everywhere you are.
How does Awareness
Grow from afar?

The Dark does exist in
True Reality.
Your Perception is
Karmic Causality.

Something, nothing and
Even everything,
Is what you make of
Becoming anything.

A place in Space, a
When unaware,
All Images caught in Time
Now where.

Nowhere is Now Here
Believe you me…
True Now is
Forever Eternity.

4. ONCE UPON A RHYME

Once you accept Who
You are,
You will Be A Shining
Star.

When you allow yourself
To simply Be,
Watch how things change
In your Reality.

When you are aware
Of Everything,
Imaginations will surely
Sing.

5. WON NOW

When you know how
You feel,
Life becomes more
Than real.

Flying up high or crawling
Down low,
Believe what you will
For you can't know...

Everything about anything
Or anything at all,
Until your complete demise, That will come before the fall.

We are all one through the Soul, of this, you may recall.
We hesitate, and we wait Sometimes we even stall.

Why deny how you feel
Doubting that it's true?
God really loves you.
Of this, you always knew.

We are one through the
Soul and won we are

Right now.
God's Love felt any Time, You need not take a bow.

One for all and won
For Now,
For me, it has been
The Tao.

6. GOD IS GRACIOUS

APPRECIATION is our way of showing GRATITUDE.

That feeling of PEACE that you RECEIVE is

GOD saying

YOU ARE MOST GRACIOUSLY WELCOME.

AMEN

7. SICUT SUPERIUS ET INFERIUS

To have FAITH in GOD is
To allow the seed of HOPE
TIME to germinate into a BELIEF
That GOD'S WILL
Be done on EARTH
As it is in HEAVEN

BELIEVING IN LOVE IS TO
BE A BEACON OF LIGHT AND
BEING A LOVING SPIRIT IS TO
BECOME A HUMAN BEING

TRUST GOD
ALL IS WELL
LOVE ALL
EVOLVE NOW

8. MYTH MATH

Math can be scary,
Math can be fun…
When you know there is
Only one.

With things in our life,
When we struggle and shout,
We are trying our best to
Figure things out.

We are masters at making
Equations we see
As complicated as can
Possibly be.

To solve our problems we
Know what to do…
Reduce your choices to
Just being two.

9. LIGHTER THAN AIR

Blood is thicker than water.
Spirit is lighter than air.
Whatever you think Matters…
Should come without cares.

Believe it or not, all Truth
LIvES in your mind.
The truth doesn't have to
Hurt…it's always kind.

All information is partially True…
What you think you can Know, you never knew.

Clearing your vision,
You'll become less dense.
With a lucid view, things
Just make more sense.

When you are lighter,
You shall fly higher…
When you glow brighter
You will inspire.

10. A PRESENT NOW

HAVE THE MOST PRESENT NOW EVER…

FROM NOW ON AND
FOREVER

YOUR DREAMS ARE YOURS TO REALIZE

YOUR FEARS WILL
 MATERIALIZE

LET GO
LET GOD

BE ALL YOU CAN BE

DROP THE FACADE
AND YOU WILL SEE

MAINTAIN A VISION
OF WHO YOU ARE

MANIFEST YOUR
REALITY

PRAISE AH

LOVE ALL
FEAR NOT

FREE YOUR SPIRIT AND
SIMPLY BE

11. FEEL FREE

Feel Free and simply be
A being living easily
Who wants nothing
But all knowing
Truth it's felt willingly.

Breathing, drinking, eating,
Sleeping...
All while freely
Perceiving.

Life is what you make it so
Letting go, allowing flow
Will show the way
For us to know.

12. WIRED WEIRD

Wired is just weird
Spelled differently,
Each being unique
In this reality.

Left is right and
Up is down,
A smile is an upturned
Frown.

How one views the
World that they feel.
Determines what
Is truly real.

I may just be odd,
I might even be strange,
To wish for variety
Of such a range.

I feel everything deeply
This way and that,

I follow my heart wearing
Quite a few hats.

Perception is the name
Of the game,
Mind and body are
One and the same.

13. DREAMS OF TREES

The dreams of these
Peaceful beings Trees,
Are visions that put
My mind at ease.

What do they feel as the
Wind moves their leaves?
Worrying never of
What they'll achieve.

We breathe, are in motion,
And try as we might
To do something
Simple as seeing the light.

All that matters is how
We are feeling
When we are simply
Humanly being.

In the span of three
Minutes of time,
We may feel how the
Trees are Divine.

They know the way
Back home to the One,
For light above is
God through the Sun.

PART FOUR

HOW WE FEEL

CHAPTER ONE

WORDS ARE POWERFUL

1. WHAT ARE YOUR THOUGHTS ON FEELINGS?

I have a theory that Feelings are the most effective form of communication. I use my Imagination to create and design ways to test all of my theories. I begin my thought experiments with one belief...

ANYTHING IS POSSIBLE

The Feelings Theory began as a hypothesis in which a brilliant logician, who happens to be a childhood friend since the age of 8, declared that Math is the only true Universal Language. I agreed that numbers are always true. I can't claim that numbers do not lie because that implies that numbers possess Consciousness. To lie is a conscious act of deception to manipulate the mind of another.

My friend explained that all beliefs are paradoxical. I saw the truth in this assertion and realized that only God can know all. Hence the attribute of Omniscience. A belief is always only partially true as the Absolute Truth can only be known to The One.

Interestingly enough, when I asked my friend if he believed in God, he stated that he does not believe in God but thought that it is a possibility. Most logical thinkers require observable evidence to completely accept anything as something that they *know to be true.*

I hypothesized that Feelings are an equally valid form of communication as math. As I explained my rationale, my friend somewhat chastised me as being too emotionally attached to my beliefs.

My friend became a bit untethered in his assertion that I was using words to prove my points. I reminded him that I was using math as words are composed of a series of letters and that a letter is a symbol that represents a sound. Any given letter, regardless of the language, has, at minimum, a specific arrangement of lines and shapes that add character to a word. These lines and shapes are arranged within set parameters of angles and lengths. They have the aspect of Geometry, which is a mathematical attribute. We see this when some letters are silent. Most letters also possess a specific sound as well. Sound can be detected and measured. Sound has seven basic qualities: pitch, tone, timbre, texture, rhythm, duration, and volume. All of these attributes can be measured. So words are mathematical at their foundational core.

Instead of allowing my friend to discourage me, I decided to make a conscious effort to better understand things from his perspective. I reopened my logical hemisphere and got back to work. I started with $E=mc^2$ the most elegantly simple equation currently known by Mankind. Albert Einstein published this equation on September 27, 1905. It showed the direct relationship between Energy and Matter. From my point of view, I naturally figured that everything in the Universe is contained in this equation. This includes Consciousness.

If all forms of matter can be observed, and Consciousness cannot yet be measured, then Consciousness must be on the "E" side of the equation. Furthermore...the stronger the power of the Energy, the faster it oscillates. The faster something oscillates, the shorter the wavelength and smaller the waveform becomes. The reason we cannot see radiation past the visible light spectrum is due simply to the size and rate of frequency being beyond what the naked eye can detect.

Upon realizing that Electromagnetic Energy continues to radiate, we can observe the effects that it has on other forms of Energy and Matter. We can assume that even though Consciousness cannot currently be observed, we can experience the effects of Consciousness. The effects of Consciousness are Reality. How do we know if we are experiencing anything at all? We don't. We believe we are because of how we feel. We are simply being aware of our feelings by becoming conscious. We Become conscious of our Awareness and are Being aware of our Consciousness.

1=Consciousness
0=Awareness
1=Cause
0=Effect
1=Becoming
0=Being

So...even if we cannot yet measure Consciousness, we can use the Zeroth Law of Thermodynamics to make sense of all of this.

A=Energy
B=Consciousness
C=Feelings

$$A$$
$$\nearrow \searrow$$
$$C \Leftarrow B$$

What becomes clear is the relationship between what we observe, how we observe it, and how that observation makes us feel.

Energy is information. Knowledge is power, so Energy is necessary for the transformation of anything in one state of being to exist in another state of being. Take a piece of *solid* matter and introduce heat. That material melts and turns into a liquid state. Heat it further, and it turns into a gaseous state.

If Energy is information, then it fuels the processing of matter. Things exist because of the ability of Energy to process things from one state to another. If that matter is a living organism, then its purpose becomes being conscious. What is the point of being conscious? It would seem that anything is conscious because it wishes to experience existing. The only reason why anything would want to exist is simply because of how it feels.

We get so caught up in the Who, What, When, Where, and How questions that we never seem to arrive at the biggest question of all… *WHY?* My favorite answer to most Why questions is… *WHY NOT?*

A more serious answer is that living feels amazing! Can life be painful? Yes, however…life can become whatever we believe it can be.

We can perceive our existence however we wish. We can create our Reality by altering our Consciousness through our Imagination. We can inspire others to express themselves however they are compelled to do while being mindful of the Free Will of others. We can use our Feelings to guide us. We can experience whatever we want, realizing that Causality is always present.

As for Math vs. Feelings, which form of communication is more effective and which one is more efficient? For logical thinkers, mathematics is the most efficient way to obtain information because it makes the most sense to that type of Consciousness.

For intuitive thinkers, written language is quite an effective form of communication, as it makes sense to them. Spoken language takes on even more effectiveness as Sound adds emotional content to the message as one's passion can be felt.

Feelings become the most effective, efficient, and informative type of communication.

Every Sentient Being makes decisions based on how they feel about their Reality. Feelings fuel our Belief System. All Beings make Free Will choices because of how they feel about whatever they believe is happening to them. Their level of Faith allows them to accept the belief that whatever is occurring is Reality.

"Cogito, ergo sum."
-René Descartes

We exist because we are conscious. We are aware of our feelings.

I AM BEING AWARE

2. HOW DO YOU FEEL ABOUT FREE WILL?

In the Spring of 2020, my childhood friend was excited about a theory he developed regarding Determinism. He stated that he can prove that only Determinism exists. Having always believed in Free Will, I was not quite ready to disband my beliefs about Free Will. I also kept in mind my friend's assertion that beliefs are all paradoxical. My friend told me that I wasn't ready to believe his Theory because I hated the idea that Free Will does not exist.

Well...I learned how to change my beliefs including accepting levels of beliefs about Determinism. I felt Peaceful for a month or so believing that Determinism does exist. I temporarily changed my belief about Free Will and accepted that only Determinism existed. I just changed Determinism to be God's Will. That made sense to me and allowed that belief to remain fairly constant for a month or so.

At this point, I was back to believing that Free Will not only exists, but it co-exists with Determinism. It became clear to me that the biggest point of contention for Determinism is specifically related to God being Omniscient. How can God know everything but allow us to have Free Will?

Everything is a matter of Perception.

If God knows *Everything,* that would include every choice we make or will make. This is exactly why we are not to judge anyone or anything. We assess and analyze because we are curious and wish to experience variety. When we do so without expectations or assumptions of any kind, we can more easily accept all occurrences as simple experiences within our Reality.

I begin all thought experiments with the simple premise…

ANYTHING IS POSSIBLE

I hypothesized that Free Will exists. My theory turned into Free Will and God's Will co-existing. As with everything ever experienced in Reality, each being has observed their unique Reality based upon their perceptions. Your perception shapes your Belief System, which inspires your Imagination. Your feelings fuel your Emotions, which further process the information.

Each thought, action, word uttered, step taken, emotion felt, and experience that has ever occurred to you is either the cause or effect due to a choice that set off a chain of events...reactions that ripple out into the Universe. Your Consciousness chooses from a series of thoughts. Each thought comes from your subconscious mind. You either hold onto a thought or delete it. Any given thought can become an idea or concept. A thought is a mental image that takes shape in your Imagination.

All of these images are memories, as they go from being a present moment occurrence to an imprinted part of your past at the exact point in time that you see that image in your mind. The longer you maintain these images in your present state of being, the greater the chance of manifesting your idea into an actual occurrence.

The one thing that maintains the frequencies is your feelings. The feelings that are most easily recognized are your emotions. It is through your emotions that take your thoughts from primal forms into distinctive images. The more clarity your idea has, the more believable it becomes. All of your Conscious States of Being (Mental, Physical, and Emotional) are in a harmoniously symbiotic relationship. If you choose thoughts or actions that throw any of your States of Being off, you become unbalanced and will spend Energy becoming centered again.

Every single occurrence that you have ever experienced can be traced back to a conscious thought that set off a series of other thoughts. Those thoughts generate other experiences that cause you to believe in something. Whenever you think that you are disbelieving in something, you are believing at the smallest degree possible for that idea to have a chance to occur.

As you become more aware of your ability to manifest your ideas from mere thoughts into actual occurrences, your Belief System expands. You begin to believe that you can achieve anything you wish. Your ideas turn into visions and before you know it, you are Living Your Dreams.

As you accept the responsibility of the power of your Consciousness, you become more aware of who and what you are. As you become more conscious of your abilities, you believe in yourself more and more. With the further development of your Belief System, you have a series of Realizations that turn into Revelations, including that you do have Free Will after all.

While you are using your Will to alter your Consciousness, you are creating your Reality. Whenever you choose to doubt something, you are believing in your ability to determine an outcome. If you believe in something strongly enough, you become so certain of its occurrence that you make it happen. You draw it into existence. If you ask another if they believe that anything is possible, there is either a resounding *"YES"* or there is a hesitation, or *"yeah, but..."* which indicates that they are determined to not fully believe in the premise that...

ANYTHING IS POSSIBLE

Most humans restrict themselves by allowing fears to dictate their beliefs. Although their fears are reasonable or even rational, they accomplish one thing...the disallowance of acceptance of the truth that each human has many things going for them and that is the ability to determine their destiny. You draw whatever you Feel the Strongest. Most play this game of accomplishment and what is perceived as defeat. What becomes clear as your Awareness expands is that when you think you fail, you proved to yourself that you made that experience occur to you. You made it happen. You determined it by choosing a series of thoughts that led to specific actions that caused other interactions to occur. You have experienced the co-existence of Determinism and Free Will.

Since God knew what choices you would make, the planning was done in God's Imagination at the point of your origin. From your perspective, you were in control the entire time. The existence of God's Plan existed concurrently with your Dreams or you would not have experienced what occurred to you. As you fostered those ideas through your Belief System, you deserved to feel whatever emotions you experienced because cause and effect are always in play.

Since everything is based upon your perception, you will either believe in the existence of Free Will or not. You can choose to believe only in Determinism or a combination of both.

I am choosing to believe in my ability to decide which occurrences will happen.

3. FORGETTING THE PAST

When we forget our past, history repeats itself. To deny any event as ever having occurred is to remain unaware of what the lesson entailed. Whenever we ignore any experience that has occurred to us, we will be ignorant of that which was being taught. Why would we need to unlearn something we already know has occurred? We can un-remember what we learned temporarily, while re-experiencing a memory, only to re-remember that which we need to use that experience as a teachable moment. To disregard anything of our past is to remain ignorant.

I feel that every experience is meant to exist or it would not have occurred. Everything is designed and planned ahead of time. This means everything serves a purpose. The purpose of all things is to exist to be an example of what can be. The perfection of this plan is found in those intricate bits of information. All Energy is information. To inform is to illuminate, which allows a thing to come into existence. Everything is a being because it is "being."

All Energy is from The One and the Singularity of The One comes from The Other. So...nothing is anything other than Pure Love. With this premise, everything is an Illusion, as nothing is ready to be Everything. The Absolute Truth of The Universe is that it is Perfectly Ordered. What is perceived as chaos, disorder, and dissonance is part of the mystery. Each chapter of our stories is a part of History.

If nothing is bad, wrong, or evil, why would we need to experience anything from that perspective? It seems evident that we repeat the lesson as many times as necessary for the concept to make sense. We require the friction of conflict to be felt exactly because we are not yet capable of understanding it logically or intuitively. This is where our Belief System is put to the test. Faith is that trust that we have in our beliefs that what we are experiencing is for our benefit, no matter what it is.

We must always be aware of the dark and respect it for the contrast that it is so that we may know the light. This process of discovery is a gift. Without pain, misery, and suffering, we learn nothing. If we knew everything, would there be any reason to live? Upon our acceptance of the purpose of life's experiences in all of their glory, wonder, horror, trials, obstacles, and triumphs, we become more aware. With the expansion of our Awareness, we recognize conflict for what it is and remind ourselves that we may freely allow ourselves to simply be.

When these Revelations occur to us, we feel Peaceful beyond measure. We realize that suffering of any type is no longer necessary, as we have become more aware of God's Pure Love. Every single lesson is a test of Faith. The lesson inherent in every single experience that has ever occurred to any living organism, or a bit of matter that has ever existed, currently exists, or will be in existence, is simple...

LOVE ALL

4. PEACEFUL WARRIOR OR FEARFUL WORRIER

We can feel however we wish about our Reality. Our feelings are drawn through our Consciousness and based on our Belief System. Everything that has ever occurred to us is specifically meant to happen or it would not have come into our Reality. We can either be a Peaceful Warrior or a Fearful Worrier.

The reason we experience such a beautiful variety of occurrences is that we inherently know that variety is the spice of life. A lot of our actions are carried out on a subconscious level before they occur in our Reality in the Present Moment. Some of our actions are seemingly self-sabotaging. We sometimes lose friends, and jobs, or have other painful experiences.

If we examine our memories closely enough, we can retrace our choices back to that one action that caused a series of other choices that led to the manifestation of that one experience that will become a Revelation. The best part of your life adventure...there are no limits to how many Revelations can occur.

The only thing that prevents any Being from Seeing the Light or Feeling Sound is resistance. The cause of resistance is a disturbance in the Force. The triggering event that begins the series of thoughts and emotions that stack up is the indicator of something we have yet to Realize beauty or have its purpose revealed to us.

For many, these igniters are events that we see portrayed in the news.

If we take any "newsworthy" event and honestly examine it, there is always a wealth of knowledge that can be absorbed. We determine the flow of information and decide the source of information for all events. If we use cable news as our source of data, we must acknowledge that all forms of media have an agenda. If we can get an idea of what the most important information is needing to be learned at that moment, we can turn our conscious attention to a more reliable source of useable data that can be trusted wholeheartedly...Mother Nature.

When we have Faith in God or however we view The Universe and tap directly into our Energy Source, we will resonate immediately. We will become into being Peacefully Sound. In this state of being, we flow more smoothly and remain receptive to a variety of forms of Energy. As long as we are flowing freely, our minds are open to new ideas and our Belief System grows.

Our creative output surges and we are compelled to be more giving, loving, and compassionate. We find more opportunities to simply perform small acts of kindness and perpetuate The Spirit by doing things from our Hearts without any burdens or expectations. We are being Peaceful Warriors and are at our most powerful level of Awareness.

When we remain resistant to becoming more aware, we live in a fearful state of being. In this state, we always attract more of the experiences that are going to seem painful. These occurrences are always intended to show us where we can further develop our Awareness, but this is not how it will be perceived. Instead of viewing these experiences as opportunities to learn, the casual observer will view these lessons as forms of suffering.

Those who suffer will believe that they are powerless in their existence. This form of survival is being in an almost constant state of worrying. The degree of worry will determine the level of stress you impose on your Mental, Physical, and Emotional States of Being. Any imbalances will cause toxic build-ups that will lead to disorder, disease, and confusion. Life as a Fearful Worrier is simply one of distress and disturbance.

When you accept your power and remain humble, you go from being in a state of dissonance to one of harmony and resonance. It is funny how we can get used to spending as much time as we do worrying and being afraid. All that is required to become a Peaceful Warrior is a willingness to learn how. When you become a willing conscious creator, you actively participate in your adventure. You will view each moment as a chance to become more illuminated. Every experience becomes a fun part of the obstacle course that you will figure out how to traverse. Being a Peaceful Warrior is fun because you are either learning how to simply be or sharing with others how to express themselves for them to also simply be.

Once you change your intentions to be a Peaceful Warrior, you will become consciously aware of how you feel in any current moment. You will view every occurrence as a learning experience that you can store as a memory. Your arsenal of teachable lessons becomes your weapons of illumination. Each being you encounter is a teacher, a student, or both. They are a Soul Sibling whether or not they are aware of that relationship. Your job as a Peaceful Warrior is to keep the peace.

The only battle that is ever fought is within. You will learn how to allow yourself to detach from those who drain your Spirit while still loving them. The defense of your Spirit is of paramount importance. When you do not pay close enough attention to how you feel, the Spirit can be easily drained. When this occurs, the battle is still not between you and the experience that drained your Spirit. Regardless of the intentions of others, the only responsibility of transmutation falls to the Peaceful Warrior. We too often forget that even those who think that they are doing you a favor are draining your Spirit whenever they discourage you from having Faith in your beliefs.

Any being that discourages you is imposing its will on yours. The challenge becomes evident when you believe that you are supposed to save those who are suffering. The truth becomes apparent. Your role is not to convince others that your way is the best way to become more aware. Your role is to simply express yourself truthfully and do so free of any fears. The ones who are tired of being miserable will pay attention and will begin to feel more peaceful almost immediately. The ones who are of The Dark Forces will fight you either with an outright attack or will infiltrate your circle of influence and will test your weaknesses.

Prepare your Consciousness by realizing that all of your experiences possess useful information. Tap into your instincts and intuition and trust those feelings. If someone or something feels off, steer clear. Give yourself permission to detach and reconnect with your Soul Family.

5. TRIAL BY FIRE

Trying is frying because burning is learning. Pain, conflict, and even destruction are all necessary for the process of discovery. Every experience is a Trial By Fire. Every single piece of matter that has ever existed, or will exist, ranging from quanta to a hypergiant star, was formed or they are being formed because of Friction.

Without Friction, nothing would exist. There would be only Nothingness. No things, no matter can come into Reality as a Physical Being without Friction. What exactly is Friction?

Let's examine $E=mc^2$ to discover the answer. Energy is information. Energy exists for the sole purpose of illuminating other particles. Basically...Energy is interacting with other pieces of Energy. These interactions are quite simply conversations of allowance. The primary ignition switch of a process such as a chemical reaction is one piece of Energy giving another piece of Energy the green light to change its position in the Spacetime Continuum. Think of the exchange as a hall pass...a permission slip to move. Energy is constantly moving, which causes the information to change its rate of frequency. This change in frequency is the modulation of motion through Space occurring over a period of Time.

$E=mc^2$

Energy in its state of rest becomes matter through the process of moving.

Energy=Data
Matter=Reformed Energy
Time=Duration of Motion
Space=Distance of Motion
Friction=Degree of Viscosity

Each piece of Energy has a signature frequency or identification of its Splace in the Universe...its point in The Space-Time Continuum. This identifying mark gives the piece of Energy its value. Without Friction, there is only Pure Consciousness without anything for that Consciousness to observe. Reality is therefore a Physical Expression of Pure Consciousness. So...Friction is necessary for Pure Consciousness to experience its Awareness. The function of Awareness is to Feel. All that we have to Realize our Consciousness is the Awareness of how we Feel. Consciousness causes the effect of Awareness.

    1=Consciousness
    0=Awareness
    1=Cause
    0=Effect
    1=Friction
    0=Feeling

The initial inspiration for the creation of The Universe was caused by the sheer terror of The One being alone in Time & Space. Without that horrifying Realization, The Revelation of God would not have occurred. Who other than God could have imagined such an amazing and intricately designed creation called The Cosmos? This name has the clue built into its sound.../cauz-mohs/.

God's Consciousness is the cause of most. We have been blessed with the same gift of Consciousness and have the ability to perceive Reality however we wish. We cause our Reality to occur.

6. ABSOLUTION THROUGH WATER

Every problem that has ever existed has a solution. The problem can always be solved, no matter how complicated the issue seems to be. Each concept being better understood poses a question. Regardless of how complicated the question is or how the equation is formulated, the truthful answer is absolving. Before finding the answer to any question, we can reduce the confusion through reduction. The Truth is Absolution.

Begin by changing how you view your problem. Think of your problem as a riddle that you will solve. Each word of the riddle is a concept that possesses a hint or piece of the puzzle that you are putting back together. A riddle is a mathematical equation. Words and numbers represent a concept or idea. To solve any equation, we can make things more simplified by reducing each side of the equation as much as possible to a meaning that makes the most sense. The most significant equation of Human History up until this point in Time is $E=mc^2$. Although there is a disconnect between classical Physics and Quantum Mechanics, Einstein's theories regarding Space, Time, and Gravity gave us a foundation from which to work. Scientists can use $E=mc^2$ as a means to compare and contrast the behavior of any form of Electro-magnetic Energy. Tying all of the known Forces together will occur someday in a Unified Field Theory.

In math, every number can be reduced to either a 1 or a 0. Math is a means of measuring logical information. This information provided logically are concepts called thoughts. There are an infinite amount of numbers that can represent things. One number, in particular, provides the answer to how anything can come into existence. That number is Pi.

This magical number is approximately equal to 3.14159. It trails off into infinity and answers one question…

What is reality?

The number solves the mystery of the ratio of a circle's circumference to its diameter. We view a circle as being perfect and yet we do not find perfect circles in nature. They do exist in a two-dimensional space but must be an illusion, as that ratio has no end. Pi is a real number and also is irrational. It is considered a Transcendental Number. Therefore, Reality is an illusion that is occurring. It might seem irrational but is infinite and real.

The answers will come through a simple Realization in which a conscious human will make that one connection after much blood, sweat, and tears. All that is required is Time, Energy, and conscious thought. This is how we solve issues that we are having in our Mental State of Being.

Concerning our Physical State of Being, all issues that arise present themselves as illnesses, disease, or disorders. All of these maladies are created to be trials. This may sound cruel and unnecessary, but there is a reason for everything that has ever occurred to every being that has ever existed. We have become so afraid of dying or suffering that we have become dependent on pharmaceutical drugs.

In the Spiritual realm of feelings, words are used to describe intuitive concepts we call emotions. These emotions are the processors of the information that arise as thoughts. The emotional content of thoughts gives the conscious thinker a means to assess the purpose of those thoughts. Every emotion has a certain frequency bandwidth. We are subconsciously drawing the emotions that we need to feel, not necessarily those that we think we want to feel.

We can tell ourselves we wish to be happy, but if we continue to cause others harm, guess how we will feel.

When we pay attention to those emotions, especially the troubling ones we have Realizations. Those AH-HA moments in which we cry are the most revealing. The Realizations turn into Revelations into which we dig deep. When this occurs, we are flooded with an ocean of emotions that come in waves. We laugh, we cry, we ponder, and we become more aware than we ever thought possible. The answers become clear through the cleansing of the way. Our tears absolve us because water is a solvent. It dissolves toxins and cleans your field of view, physically washing away debris around your eyes, and breaking down resistance within. When we remain fearful and angry, we are resisting the truth to infuse us with the light.

When we become more aware of the Absolute Truth, we simply wash away all burdens. We become physically lighter as become enlightened. There is nothing that cannot be solved. There are no questions that can't be answered through The Truth in Light and Absolution of Love. By doing two things, you will resolve all confusion, and absolve all burdens…

JUST BREATHE
AND HYDRATE
EVERY DAY

7. INNOCENCE FOUND

We begin our lives as purely innocent Beings. We do not have even close to the degree of Awareness or rate of Consciousness that equals that which we are currently experiencing. For our first year of existence, we exist for the Soul Purpose of simply being loved by our caretakers. Those who love us unconditionally feel that Love and experience immeasurable Peace and Joy whenever they appreciate the interactions with you during this stage of your life.

Our existence serves one purpose. It does not matter how long we live and regardless of what we do with our lives. The purpose of our life is not dependent on what degree of Awareness we experience or the rate of Consciousness we attain. We can either achieve whatever we wish and feel Peaceful or be miserable thinking that the Universe is out to get us. By simply existing, we are serving The Prime Directive, which is to simply Be.

No matter what you do during your childhood, you maintain your innocence the entire time. Some enjoy a longer period of this innocence than others. Some experience only the pure bliss of absolute unawareness before being born and nothing of a human infant or child. The duration of time for each human's period of innocence can be altered by another being. This is an imposition of their will over the innocent Being's Free Will. The draining of another's Spirit occurs whenever a Being is told to stop believing in fairy tales, or that unicorns exist, or hearing that all too damning curse...*GROW UP!*

Each of us is rediscovering how fun it was to be childlike. How much fun did we have as kids playing with our friends and family members? Do you remember the anticipation of hearing the bell that indicated that it was time for recess? Do you recall those moments when you just laughed at nothing in particular? How free did you feel playing well into the evening hours during the summer months? Did you enjoy using your imagination when you used your box of crayons to color? How much fun did you have getting up early on Saturday mornings to watch cartoons?

If nothing of which I speak resonates with you, then I pray for the day that will come when you do remember how fun life can be. If you were ignored, neglected, abused, or bullied so much that your childhood experience was extinguished too soon, I pray for you to recall even one moment in which you felt joy and love. If your innocence was so destroyed that your inner child crawled into the darkness and is still in hiding...allow yourself to be found.

When you rediscover your joy of childhood innocence, you will laugh again. You will heal all of the past traumas that occurred to you by simply going back out to recess and playing once again. Just like learning in the classroom takes time, so does re-learning how to play as you did as a five-year-old. No matter how old you are when you find your innocence, be patient with yourself and allow yourself to feel whatever emotions you are going to feel. You will recollect moments that will cause you to laugh as well as cry. You may remember an incident in which you were bullied or maybe severely beaten or abused. Those experiences occurred and although they altered your perception of the world, you have regained control of the one thing that generates all of those beautiful ideas, dreams, emotions, visions, and other-worldly feelings... *YOUR IMAGINATION.*

Once you reclaim your Imagination, there is nothing that can stop you from creating whatever you wish. Your Belief System will re-expand into those fantasy realms where unicorns re-appear. You will feel free to simply be a kid again living fearlessly and invulnerably. In our Imagination, we need not worry about wasting time, as we have an infinite supply of it We need not concern ourselves with you occupying any particular space as there is an unlimited amount of Space. We do not have to fear anything, as there is an immeasurable array of experiences yet to discover. The only thing we ever have to pay attention to is Our Spirit.

Upon re-remembering how to truly play, have fun, laugh, and enjoy life, we no longer have to spend time in detention or having a time-out. Anyone and I mean any being who discourages you from proceeding on your Treasure Hunt, can be dismissed from class to speak to the principal. They are not doing you any favors.

Class...Time For Recess!

8. BE FREE TO FEEL HOWEVER YOU WISH

I believe our greatest gift is Awareness. Through our Awareness, we feel everything. We feel our Consciousness, physical reality, emotions, thoughts, and memories. We can even feel our Awareness by being aware of our Consciousness and perceiving ourselves.

The greatest gift we have is Free Will. Our ability to choose what we wish to experience, create, perceive, think, say or do is summed up in one term...Feeling. We not only choose how we feel about whatever we choose to experience, but we can also choose to feel however we wish about how we feel about the process of feeling. Becoming more aware of just how Free you are is truly an amazing and awe-inspiring experience.

When you feel free, you are in the perfect position to receive pure love from all sources of Energy because you are aware that all information comes from The One, which is born of The None. Any confusion as to the source of All Love is merely evidence that you are simply misunderstanding the intentions of The One. All misunderstandings, misgivings, and misinterpretations are already forgiven because there is only God's Will to Love you unconditionally.

Practicing how to use our Free Will is a beautiful form of meditation. As your Awareness expands, you will be feeling more of everything, including emotions, thoughts, and physical sensations. With supreme levels of Faith, we can navigate through this obstacle course of Conscious Expansion of Awareness by re-remembering how to simply let things move in the waves that they ebb and flow.

The only way to truly feel free is to remind yourself that there are no such things as improper thoughts, bad emotions, or evil feelings. There is only Love that The Universe is offering to All Beings. Any lack of clarity comes from a breakdown in communication between the sender and receiver of the information. These miscommunications are always understandable, and even reasonable in most situations. The question you can ask yourself is whether or not the conversation has the potential to proceed civilly. Whether your interaction continues or not, you win either way as you will become more aware of something about yourself and the being with whom you are communing.

Feeling free is so liberating in so many ways that you become more aware of every aspect of your being. Because of this feeling, you have less resistance to obtaining information from all sources. By allowing yourself to absorb more information, you sense more than you ever have before. You become conscious of Senses that you didn't even realize you had.

With a sense of freedom, all possibilities open up, and as your conscious rate of frequency increases. As your Awareness expands, you become more lucid. With more lucidity, your visions become crystal clear. With focused clarity, all questions dissolve into solutions.

Being truly free means your imagination can run wild without the care of what others will think about your creative ideas. You will no longer be afraid to express how you feel. You will not worry about what others will say about your beliefs. You will no longer feel the urge to destroy, fight, argue, or debate. You will only wish to create.

I AM AWARE OF
HOW FREE I FEEL

9. MISuNderStandIngs - MISINterpretationS - MISgIviNgS

What's the only thing that's missin' in any communication, conversation, or interaction?

The only thing that matters, is a deeper understanding of the concept being presented. All misunderstandings cause misinterpretations and misgivings. Misunderstandings occur because the information is being misinterpreted or is misconstrued and doubted.

Misinterpreted data is sometimes caused by the data itself being corrupted. If the one doing the transmitting intends to deceive, discourage, or destroy, then that message will either cause further discord and dissonance or will be interpreted clearly. If you realize that all experiences are originating from The One, then you will discover the useful portions of the information as partially true. If you judge the process harshly and are unaware of the Divine Origin of the message, you will misinterpret the data and become confused. That level of understanding will remain within that frequency range until you change your tune by altering your perception consciously. In other words, you will need to modulate the rate of your Consciousness.

Any misgivings that you have are doubts about the validity of the information. These doubts are caused by your current level of Awareness in which you are consciously judging the being who is channeling the message. The level of judgment is commensurate with the level of judgment you reflect right back onto yourself.

The communication breakdown occurs along the chain of information the moment you determine that the data is lacking any viable information. Keep in mind that all experiences that occur to you are meant to happen to you exactly how they are presented or they would not occur at all. How do you perceive any experience? Does it matter if the event that occurs is known ahead of time or unforeseen?

I view every single experience that has ever occurred to me as a valuable lesson. If you view anything that happens as a form of punishment, you will suffer. If you realize that everything is a conversation between your Consciousness and God's Consciousness, then you will never suffer again.

Sometimes the learning process is painful, but the level of pain is commensurate with the level of awareness that will occur to you. The higher the degree of pain you feel, the greater the sense of urgency you will feel to absorb the information. Realizing that there is no problem at all, and not even an issue that needs to be resolved, but only a riddle that will be solved. The answer is the solution and all answers already exist or the riddle would not have been presented.

Regardless of how, when, or where the dissonance occurs, all confusion can and will be cleared up and the being who was cloudy of vision becomes more lucid. The phrase '*more will be revealed*' is a clue to what is occurring to each being.

Any Other feelings Than Peaceful (OTP) only ever signal from the Divine Spirit that will give you but a moment to pause. Only when you ignore the signs are you disallowing your infusion of new information to be downloaded. Ignorance is not bliss; immeasurable peacefulness and pure love are blissful. Ignorance is allowing yourself to remain at whatever level of Awareness that is occurring at the moment in which you currently feel. If you wish to experience more of that feeling, remain as aware as you wish. If you wish to become more aware, allow yourself to accept more information and assess your Spirit level as you process the influx of Conscious Energy and Waves of Sound. Your level of Peacefulness grows with the expansion of Awareness.

Feelings are amorphic and can present themselves in so many different ways. Feelings are not observed. Feelings are sensed through various Earthly Senses. Feelings adhere to thoughts, emotions, images, concepts, and ideas. Feelings are the Spirit Guides that show us the way. All cloudiness is cleared away as the path presents itself.

10. SIMULTANeOuS SIMULATiONS

Throughout Human History, we could learn how things work. We use feelings as our guides. All information is obtained via our feelings and processed through our Consciousness. How we perceive our Reality is based upon what we believe. Our entire Belief System is founded on how we feel about those thoughts, ideas, and notions about whatever is occurring to us. The biggest question for many is...*WHY ARE WE HERE?*

We believe that if we answer the Who, What, When, and Where questions, we will solve the Why questions. Science is very focused on the How questions. Instead of viewing the task of learning as a means to feel more Peaceful, the logical thinker believes that with knowledge comes power.

KNOWLEDGE IS POWER
WISDOM IS PEACEFUL

One possibility of how our Universe functions were brought forth in the 1999 film *The Matrix*. The idea of our world being a holographic simulation ignited my imagination. Science fiction did its job by inspiring other creative humans to think outside of the box. Renowned physicists like S. James Gates, who is a huge Sci-fi fan, also believes that our Universe is a simulation. Professor Gates uses math to study Supersymmetry, Supergravity, and Superstring Theory.

So...we currently have scientists and artists that hold a similar belief. Before we create ways to prove how something works, we are inspired to create an idea or concept. If the idea is inspiring, we go from a state of just wanting to believe it can occur to desiring this so much that we are compelled to either prove it already exists or can become a part of our Reality.

If the idea causes enough anxiety, we become afraid of it already existing, or that it can potentially become an actual occurrence. This notion becomes a dilemma that we will set out to solve by disproving that it exists or can exist in our Physical Reality.

If we accept that anything can possibly exist, then we can spend our time more wisely by better understanding it instead of trying to determine its non-existence or limiting perception of that concept. We ask more of the Why questions and are more easily able to come up with formulas that explain the relation between A and B.

I am a natural philosopher who discovers how things work by asking why questions. The how answers come through a series of data absorptions. I analyze the data by processing the information through my Consciousness and assessing its value based on how I feel about the answers. In other words...I find ways for it to simply make sense.

The notion of us being trapped in a computer-generated system can illicit much anxiety. The idea that we can be enslaved in any manner is daunting. So instead of viewing yourself as being trapped in a prison of sorts, you can view your Universe as your home in which you are free to roam Wherever you wish, and Whenever you are willing to change your position while modulating this Time and Space in Whatever way you wish it to occur.

If you understand how a system operates, you can learn how to access the very information that you seek. This most useful information is going to be that which is the most liberating. The more freedom you can realize that is accessible through the absorption of data, the more fun you will enjoy.

ARE WE IN A MATRIX?

Yes, we are, but start with the word "matrix" and know that it is derived from the Latin word "mater," which is mother. Think of the Physical Realm as a motherboard of circuits that we are uploaded into as programs. Each conscious program is a simulation. Each of the 8 billion different Consciousnesses are simulated programs that are co-existing…

SIMULTANeOuS
SIMULATiONS

The only thing that changes over time is your rate of Conscious Frequency (Consciousness) and your degree of feeling (Awareness). In the 1999 film *The Matrix*, Morpheus gets Thomas Anderson's attention through his computer. Initially, Mr. Anderson is doubting Thomas. He doubts that the Agents are the bad guys and is unaware of his actual state of being in which he is in a life-sustaining and life-force draining cocoon used to tap into his Electro-magnetic Energy.

As Neo meets other humans who have escaped that primary source of enslavement, he begins to wonder what is going on because he is not yet aware that their initial contact and interactions are in The Matrix. Because Neo is naturally curious, he becomes the proverbial Adam by choosing the red pill (Fruit of Knowledge). Neo's role changes upon the recognition of where he had been his whole current lifetime. Morpheus the prophet character believes in his vision with enough faith that he offers Neo the idea that he is the One. It occurs to Neo that he might be the One. Taking on the Messiah role made sense to Neo, but only enough for him to continue the training with Morpheus.

Hopefully, you have seen this brilliant and ground-breaking film. If you haven't, do your imagination a favor and watch, listen, and feel illuminated. I believe we are in a Matrix not just because of this film, but after experiencing 21 years of life observing how we have been programmed to believe what we think is occurring and bypassing how we feel because of what we are taught.

We are conditioned to believe that we are supposed to control our Emotions. We are told to stop acting like a child. We are taught to completely ignore our feelings and can only learn from what we observe or hear. We forsake all of our other Senses and are shamed into thinking that we are not supposed to enjoy things like eating, sex, or being creative because we will become addicted to those natural processes of life. We are so controlled by fear that we comply with restrictions on the most basic of natural rights...breathing. We are indoctrinated into the idea that we better worship God in a certain way or else we will go to Hell and not just for a while, but for an Eternity!

We are conditioned to fear death so much that we agree to do things we would not otherwise do. Please note that I do not blame any being for the confusion and simple misunderstanding that has caused all of the anxiety. We all have had plenty of experiences that have given us just cause to worry, doubt, and live in various states of panic. I understand the fear because I have felt everything from seeds of doubt to abject terror. All degrees of fear make sense and are completely rational until that fear no longer serves its purpose. When being afraid no longer makes sense, begin your new life. You know how to survive. You have learned how to live. When you re-remember how to truly thrive...you will be as you were as a child playing.

Living fearlessly is simply more fun. The feeling of liberation is indescribable. The moment of Revelation in which you no longer are burdened by Anything is when your actual reason for living begins. Causality still is in play, but as you become fully Realized, you will no longer wish to cause harm to anyone. You will love all with a compassionate heart, keeping an open mind, while enjoying a free Spirit.

CHAPTER TWO

FEELING YOUR SENSES

1. HOW DO WE SENSE THINGS?

The Universe speaks in many different frequencies of Energy. The Universe is designed to be sending messages in an array of Frequencies. $E=mc^2$ so everything is in play because everything is in a constant yet modulating state of motion. Even the Void of Nothingness is a moving entity.

Energy serves one purpose...to signal a command. The commands are very simple...begin to be or remain to be. We are no longer required to view these commands as True/False, On/Off, or even Go/Stop. There is either Becoming or Being.

1=Becoming
0=Being

There are Two Fundamental Forms of Communication occurring between any Being, Thing, or Entity.

Light Forms
Sound Forms

Light signals beings and things when it is time to move or begin a chemical reaction. All sorts of chemical reactions occur throughout nature, each with a specific purpose. All Light Forms communicate that it is time for one thing to Become Something else.

Sound Forms make all of the difference in the world. Sound moves air, which causes changes in the pressure being exerted. These forces matter to move or take shape and create new formations. Sound affects our Mental State of Being by compelling us to move our bodies, which elicits an emotional response, and also releases endorphins. Sound Forms communicate that it is time to simply Be Something.

Electro-Magnetic Energy is how all frequencies are transmitted and communicated from The Source to all things in the Universe. When electrons change position, they transform the energy by forming an ion.

Ionization is one of the principal ways that radiation, such as charged particles and X-rays transfers its energy to matter. The process of photoionization occurs when photons are emitted from electrons and give off radiation. During photosynthesis in green plants, light energy is captured and used to convert water, carbon dioxide, and minerals into oxygen- and energy-rich organic compounds.

Every single bit of data is a piece of vital information. Every bit of information is a piece of light. Each bit of light illuminates the Space around where that illumination is occurring. Interaction is made possible through these transmissions of data. The interactions cause other processes to occur, whether they be through heat induction, chemical reactions, or ionization. All of these interactions are transferences of Energy. One thing becomes another.

With Sound Forms, there is an initial transfer of Energy. Those particles move air, which reforms matter by inducing a change in the position of particles, which in turn affects other particles. The particles are not shown what to Become but instead are being allowed to simply refrain from changing further. In other words, they are feeling that it is time to simply Be in whatever state is occurring at that moment. Something Becomes a Being.

These interactions between molecules cause chemical reactions to occur. Some of these chemical reactions include the release of endorphins in our bodies. Endorphins are released during times of stress, pain, or toxicity. Endorphins are also released during activities such as sex, eating, meditation, or exercising. The endorphins cause the effects of sensory input we call pleasure.

All experiences are opportunities for us to either Become more enLIGHTened or Be as AH-where as we are currently being. Every moment in time is occurring in your Reality. Your Consciousness observes these occurrences through your unique perception, which is capable of changing as will all aspects of your being. You will believe whatever you choose to believe in based on your perspective, which is the angle at which your perception is viewing each occurrence. As Beliefs change, they are never entirely dispelled. They are temporarily disbanded as any dissonance becomes unnecessary in the learning process. That does not mean that you will always be unable to understand that Being or experience. A Divinely inspired reunion with every unresolved issue will reappear in due time.

Become What You Are Meant To Be. Allow yourself to feel Peaceful.

2. OUR EIGHT EARTHLY SENSES

(SIGHT)

Our Sense of Sight is dependent on photons being observed through time. Those Illuminated particles are signals. They are ignition switches. These signifiers are communicating a command telling other particles that it is time to change their position. That change in their point in the Space-Time Continuum is when one thing becomes another thing. Electro-magnetic Frequencies within the Visible Spectrum are sensed through our eyes.

Those observable frequencies are photons moving in waves. Photons serve one purpose. They are generated to be observed. The photons hit the light-sensitive tissue in the eye called the retina. Photoreceptor cells transform the photons into electrical signals. Those signals are transmitted along the optical nerve to the brain where those signals are transformed into images.

The most useful information is absorbed and imprinted into our brain cells. These imprints are stored data we call memories.

We can recall and review these memories whenever we wish. Whatever emotions we felt upon initially experiencing that occurrence can be revealed...Re-Felt.

(SOUND)

Our Sense of Sound is experienced through the feeling of motion, which are waves of emotion.

Radio Waves can transmit Sound Waves that are occurring in one place on Earth such as a live concert very efficiently through the air. Transponders transmit those signals, which are picked up by receivers called radios, which are transducers that transfer that energy back to electrical energy and transferred further back into mechanical energy of speakers physically moving, which push air toward your ears.

All Sounds are felt through sensory receptors in our eardrums that are moved by the motion of airwaves. Our eardrums absorb those airwaves. Those vibrations are deciphered in our brain, which translates that energy to what we perceive as sound. Louder sounds that are presented at bass frequencies will be felt in our Solar Plexus. These sound waves are compressing our chest, which is felt by our hearts.

Sounds can be reproduced in our minds as well. Re-feeling sounds mentally convey meaning but are not as moving as when you hear and feel actual sound waves. The same can be said regarding music that is expressed as a notation on paper or in the digital realm. A skilled composer can hear the notes before they are played but realizes that the power of sound materializes emotional feedback.

(SMELL)

Our Olfaction System is our ability to smell. We possess sensory cells called olfactory neurons. These cells are found in a small patch of tissue high inside the nose. Molecules called odorants are absorbed into these neurons. The molecules are converted to an electrical signal and transmitted directly to the brain.

All aromas are composed of several different individual odorant molecules. We can detect and discern between one trillion different molecules. Because of the relatively huge variation of distinction, there is a greater chance of an aroma triggering a long-lasting memory than any other Sense.

Smelling pleasing aromas can have a relaxing effect. Smelling natural pheromones can have a stimulating effect on animals, causing them to actively seek out a member of the opposite sex to mate with. The jury is still out regarding humans but has some relevance as we use perfumes and colognes to attract sexual partners.

(TASTE)

Our Sense of Taste is very similar to our Sense of smell.

Our taste buds contain nerve receptors that absorb molecules of whatever we are eating. Taste receptors are chemosensory receptors that transduce molecules to generate a biological signal. These molecules are recognized into 5 different categories...

SWEET
SOUR
SALTY
BITTER
UMAMI

Three chemical senses are working together, including our Olfaction, Taste, and Trigeminal. The Trigeminal System is our ability to detect chemical compounds through our Sense of smell and Taste that are irritants, pollutants, or toxic contaminants. Wearing masks and face coverings unnecessarily diminishes that chemical detection system simply because our receptors are not getting the full message.

As for our Sense of Taste...what a pure joy. Tasting various flavors can be quite an exhilarating experience. We enjoy mixing these five types of flavors for the same reason we enjoy mixing colors. There are no limits to the array of tastes that can be created and shared with others.

(TOUCH)

Our Somatosensory System utilizes various sensory neurons to receive information called stimuli. We have thermoreceptors, which analyze thermal temperatures. We possess mechanoreceptors, which are receptors that respond to mechanical pressure or distortion. Lastly, we have nociceptors, which serve the purpose of responding to potentially damaging stimuli and relaying that information as possible threats. Our brains analyze these messages and respond by conveying the stimuli as pain. The more painful, the more damage you will incur if you do not remove the part of your body that is causing the pain.

Our Sense of Touch is quite magical. We believe that when we touch something, our fingers are touching another thing. At no point do any particles make contact when they are touching. There is resistance that is felt as repulsion on an atomic level. A combination of thermoreceptors and mechanoreceptors work together to generate what we feel is a pleasurable experience. Certain biological activities will induce the release of endorphins that intensify our sensations of pleasure.

(SPACE)

Our Sense of Space is called Proprioception. This sense allows for our ability to know which direction to move. This sense enables us to place parts of our body through spaces in which we wish to maneuver. We have proprioceptors in our muscles and tendons that tell our cells how far to move. The receptors communicate with our brain telling them how far to stretch and which direction to move. These receptors are communicating where our limbs should go. Complex mathematical equations are calculated regarding how much force to exert and which angles of direction to use.

We often believe that we only learn primarily by what we see, hear, or a combination of the Sense of Sight and Sound. We actually can learn from all of our Senses. We have been conditioned to believe only observational data or conceptual information takes precedence. Science teaches how things work. We can measure the behavior of Electro-magnetic Frequencies, the rate of fluctuation, as well as their power and the effect it has on other materials. We can learn much from our Senses of Smell, Taste, Touch, and Space. The kind of knowledge we can gather is immeasurable but certainly invaluable.

Our Senses allow us to gather data, which alters our Consciousness. This alteration changes our Perception, allowing us to experience whatever we wish. As we view our Reality differently, we become more inspired to use our Imagination creatively. As we become more aware of how we can consciously control our environment, in doing so, we enhance our Belief System. We begin to believe that we are ultimately responsible for the creation of our Reality.

(MOTION)

Our Vestibular Sense pertains to our relationship to gravity and how we feel Motion. Balancing aids in our ability to know how much pressure to exert in our legs to remain standing. When something exerts its energy against ours, causing us to become off balance, we can estimate very accurately how much force to use with our arms and torso to counteract the effects of falling off balance. We can also sense G-forces as we move faster.

(TIME)

Our Sense of Time becomes evident at an early age. Whenever we get confused or frustrated, we are feeling the Force of Friction through Linear Time. Time seems to fly when we are having fun, but does Time actually move faster, or do we only feel like it does? Each Being can alter its Sense of Time. We realize that we can have fun whenever we wish, including when we are feeling friction. Think about the last time you smashed your elbow. The reason it is called the *"funny bone"* is that you laugh, even though it smarts. Laughing causes the release of endorphins, which counteracts the painful aspect of that experience. Whenever we laugh, Linear Time becomes irrelevant. When we judge our experiences as a form of punishment, we determine how long we are going to suffer. During these experiences, what occurs to us is the slowing down of Time.

We set our internal clocks. We have Free Will, which allows us to choose what thoughts we wish to foster into ideas. We choose how we will spend our Time.

We can use our Sense of Time in conjunction with our Sense of Space and Motion to estimate the distance covered.

The more of our senses we use together, the more we can evaluate various aspects of the experiences that occur in our reality.

3. SINES, SIGNALS, SYMBOLS, SYNCHRONICITIES

(T)ransformation occurs by
(A)bsorbing
(O)servable light

There is only truth in the Light as it all comes from The One Source. There are no sins, mistakes, accidents, or coincidences. There are only Sines, Signals, Symbols, and Synchronicities.

Electro-magnetic Radiation is how anything that exists, in Reality, is observed. In 1801, Thomas Young showed that Light can be observed as behaving as particles or moving in a wave. The shape of these EM Waves is sinusoidal (Sine Waves). The EM Spectrum covers the whole range of measurable Energy. For the time being, which is NOW, we will focus on visible light. Five colors make up the visible spectrum:

Black
White
Yellow
Red
Blue

We are familiar with blends of these colors:
Black+White=Gray
Yellow+Red=Orange
Red+Blue=Purple

We have gradient variations, as well as degrees of saturation. When we combine depth, textures, and shapes, we process all of that information.

We can learn from observing this information. Concepts can be expressed in written symbols and viewed on some sort of parchment typed out and viewed on a screen from the digital realm. Either way, we are viewing compressed data. We are not viewing individual photons, but rather a culmination of these particles that form an image. To make sense of the image, we view it from a point in space that accepts the data from a perspective that accounts for a summation of all of those moving parts.

In the case of symbols called letters, we view a conglomerate of letters called words. Combinations of words create phrases that become concepts and ideas. These ideas are thoughts expressed in a manner that can allow two beings to have a conversation. Words possess power, but if the phrasing is not efficiently done, the word placement can leave room for misinterpretation. When writing is translated into a different language, meaning can change causing a different perception of the message. When words are spoken with expressive passION, there is an IONizatION that occurs. Our animated being can cause others to laugh, gasp, and cry tears of gratitude.

In the case of symbols called digits, we can use these to represent an abstract idea, which describes a quantitative value called a number. A numeral is the name of that number. 101 is a numeral representing a number that is composed of two of the 1 digit, and one of the 0 digit. A single digit is composed of 4 bits of data.

```
0000=0
0001=1
0010=2
0011=3
0100=4
0101=5
0110=6
0111=7
1000=8
1001=9
```

101 requires the following series of data to be expressed in the digital realm...000100000001. As you can imagine, when we wish to express more complex shapes and colors, the amount of data required to represent that image grows exponentially. Imagine everything you have experienced up until now and how many words it would take to describe just the basics of what occurred to you during your life. That would consist of billions of bits of data.

Our ability to process these data streams and the speed at which we recognize shapes, patterns, and colors to form concepts is based upon our Intelligence Quotient.

This does not mean that being more intelligent than another makes you more aware of how you feel. I know many who are blessed with a lower-than-average IQ but are quite brilliantly Peaceful and Radiant Beings. I also know those with genius-level IQs who think that they know the Truth of Existence but are quite miserable in their Mental and Emotional State of Being. The stress of being afraid, thinking that you are supposed to know anything, will affect your Physical Well Being.

Where does that leave us? Are we supposed to not be curious? Did Adam and Eve commit any sins whatsoever?

We are left with only acceptance of the Truth In Light. It is perfectly natural to be curious about anything and everything. We are genetically engineered to specifically experience everything that occurs to us. The only difference between knowing anything and understanding it is how we feel about it. Only God is Omniscient. That does not mean we are not allowed to ever know what God knows. We were given Life, Consciousness, and Free Will for not only a purpose, or even a higher purpose, but actually for The Highest Purpose.

The Trillion Dollar question is...

Why Are We Here On Earth?

The answer...

To Become Human Beings.

How do we accomplish this possible task?

Only through accepting Who and What we are can we freely allow for information to be absorbed by simply living.

Wait...can it be that easy?

YES!

But hold on a minute...

Nothing can be that simple.

Really? Actually, yes... Everything is as simple as you need it to be for it to make sense to you. If you are ever confused about something, you have moved from analysis and assessment toward labeling and limiting. By doing so, you are determining that something is not meant for you. You have decided that there is no useful information being provided then. You have chosen to remain unaware of data that will benefit you. Let me be clear...this does NOT mean you are required to let yourself become toxic.

So now...the question becomes...

How do I know what to do?

You are not supposed to *know* anything other than how you feel Right Now!

When? Now.

How about now? Still Now...

Whenever we feel any of the Friction expressed through linear Time, we are reminded that a lesson is about to present itself. What exactly is being taught will become apPARENTly clear through Father Time.

When we accept all experiences as lessons, we become more aware of how Reality is an Illusion. This Illusion is not meant to fool or trick us. The Grand Illusion is meant to create a Foundational Framework by which we can compare and contrast what we observe.

If we judge what we view as anything other than our Reality meant specifically for us, we will suffer. Our level of Peacefulness correlates with the level of Appreciation we exhibit. If we share our gifts through expressions of art, music, or simple gratitude, we feel joy. Any acts of kindness, compassion, and love expressed without expectations of reward or assumptions of a duration of any peaceful feelings, will be a transceiver.

Everything that we see is a series of Sines, Signals, Symbols, and Synchronicities.

What will you make out of the information?

What type of Being will you Become? Will you use this data to deceive, discourage, and destroy the Spirit of Others, or will you choose to transceive, encourage, and uplift the Spirit of All You Encounter?

I KNOW WHAT I AM BEING

4. FEELING PEACEFUL BY BEING SOUND

We become more aware of our feelings as we pay attention to the present moment whenever we are conscious of our Time. When we realize that we are always in The Eternal Now, we remember that everything is perfectly sound and we are feeling as Peaceful as can be. We can either feel Peaceful or realize that we are becoming Peaceful.

Every moment in Time possesses an infinite amount of possibilities for every particle that exists. Every piece of Energy is a bit of data that can become something other than what it currently is being. Each quantum can change its position in the Universe. That change of its place in Time and Space occurs when it changes its frequency. That change in frequency is nothing more than a change in its motion. It either begins to spin in its current position, rotates around another particle, or travels through Space-Time altogether.

The One Connection between all is that everything that exists is a form of Energy. Because of this connection, the timing and position of any change to any bit of data are always perfectly ordered. Each change causes other changes to occur and ripple throughout The Universe.

We become more knowledgeable about something by what information we accept regarding it. We become more aware of anything by how we feel about it. Because of the currently limited capacity of our brains, we can only know so much at any given moment we exist as Human Beings. The number of connected neurons in our brain may determine our intelligence, but our level of awareness is based on how deeply we feel. Our Consciousness increases its rate of frequency as it accepts more illumination. With this increased enlightenment comes a better understanding of the information that was accepted. Our Awareness expands within ourselves the deeper we feel. The more attention we pay to our feelings, the more allowance for Sound Frequencies will be felt. That expansion of Awareness creates deeper innerstanding.

We determine our state of being through our feelings.

The feelings that are the most recognizable are our emotions. These types of feelings are what make our existence seem REAL. We are not our thoughts. What we think about our emotions does not truly matter. What matters the most is how we feel about anything that occurs to us. Emotions make the most sense to us because of how we decide what thoughts to hold onto. Those emotionally charged thoughts that occur to us gain our attention quickly and are quite useful as guides that offer us ways in which to perceive the experience. As our perceptions are altered, our beliefs will change naturally.

We maintain whatever beliefs we desire to remain within the conscious rate of frequency that we wish to feel. How do we know if that feeling is correct? Since we cannot know exactly how something will feel ahead of the time in which it is supposed to occur, we use our emotional feedback to test the waters as we continue on our journey of processing the information. Our feelings are how the Spirit guides us.

We very often get stuck in thought loops that do nothing but torment us. We torture ourselves because we believe that we have done something wrong. We feel guilty when we think that we have done something evil. We forget that we are becoming more human with each occurrence that we experience. With each occurrence comes enlightening information if we choose to feel it.

We can become more aware of how being Peaceful feels, not just how we expect that it will feel before it occurs. The recognition of the perfect Sound Frequencies is based on the resonant frequency of your nervous system. Each thing has a different resonant frequency, as does every Human Being. We resonate the most with others that are within a similar resonant frequency and who are being within a range of Sound frequencies that harmonize sympathetically with ours.

As we become more familiar with those particular Sound frequencies, we are going to naturally put out our feelers that will sense those beings.

We are therefore feeling Peaceful by being Sound. That state of being is consciously chosen and we become more aware of how that Sound feels. Being Peaceful is to simply Be Sound.

I AM PEACEFULLY
SOUND.

5. STOP AND SMELL THE FLOWERS

Our sense of smell is a truly mystical ability that has been gifted to us. We have been so conditioned to believe that the most useful information we obtain is done through our sense of sight and sound. We are so ready and willing to believe what we see or hear that we often disregard our other senses as being viable means of obtaining information. Being too attached to any of our Senses can lead to addiction. When we rely entirely on Sight and Sound only, we can become addicted to television or social media for our daily doses of information. It is easy to be deceived by what we see and hear because regardless of the intentions of the being who is producing the content, the information is only partially true. Our physical bodies are specifically designed to absorb information through all of our Senses.

Our sense of smell is the most mysterious of our earthly senses. Our olfactory system is made up of sensory receptors which are neurons that receive molecules called odorants. These neurons are proteins that can combine odorants that allow us to analyze the data. We can discern between one trillion different odorant molecules but can group them into 10 classes. There is only useful information in every single different odorant that we can smell. There is no deception. There is only information for us to better understand. The phrase *wake up and smell the coffee* very bluntly describes how there is much truth in what we smell.

10 Classifications of Odors

1. Fragrant
2. Fruity
3. Citrus
4. Woody and resinous
5. Chemical
6. Sweet
7. Minty
8. Toasted and nutty
9. Pungent (e.g. blue cheese, cigar smoke)
10. Decayed (e.g. rotting meat, sour milk)

Each of the 10 classifications of odorants is designed to provide valuable information. Our bodies need some of the chemicals we smell and others are not only unnecessary but potentially harmful.

The whole purpose of our sense of smell is to analyze data on a molecular level. Each significant aroma triggers a moment in time that we call a memory. The lasting effect of each memory is determined by the number of endorphins that are released if it is a pleasurable experience or the degree of irritation or nauseousness that we feel caused by smelling chemicals, pungent, or decaying matter.

Our ability to distinguish a potentially dangerous chemical through our sense of smell is a distinctive defense mechanism. Without this ability, we are susceptible to inhaling pollutants that range in degrees of harmfulness from being irritants to toxic and even deadly. This classification of odorants is the most useful in maintaining our bodies in a fully functional state of living.

Another level of defense would entail decaying matter. We may not die if we encounter decaying matter, but we can become ill. We can become ill to the point of nausea where we vomit or we can become infected with harmful bacteria. Our level of discomfort is attributed to the degree of importance that we should place on clearing away or sterilizing the area from which the foul odor emanates.

Some of the classes of smells are signaling that your body craves a certain food. I count five cross-over classes of Smells that relate to the nutritional information of things we can Taste. (Fruity, Citrus, Sweet, Minty, and Toasted/Nutty). Those types of cravings are your cells asking for certain nutritional content. That nutritional information serves to give us an idea of which chemical reactions will balance out our bodily systems.

The pungent class can include certain foods but also things like cigar smoke. This class would be providing you with information that you can fulfill a desire that is not a necessity. Sexuality is driven in animals by pungent odors that signal that the female is in heat. Most desires may not be necessary to survive in our current bodies, but offer us things to experience to become more aware. The strongest desire for many beings is our sex drive. Procreation is the best way to prolong our Consciousness as we pass down memories stored to our offspring.

Fragrant and woody/resinous classifications of aromas are signaling us to simply take time to appreciate nature. These types of aromas are the most useful in terms of experiencing levels of Peacefulness.

STOP AND SMELL THE FLOWERS

This simple act takes but a few seconds and a minimal amount of your attention. If you take time out of your day to smell beautiful aromas, you are present. When you feel stressed out or angry, when you smell anything that is beautifully aromatic, you are appreciating what nature has to offer you. A basic appreciation for simple things will calm your nerves. This
calming effect will reduce stress levels. When your mind, body, and emotions are balanced, you will find yourself being peaceful.

These peaceful moments are when you are still and when you are silent. Awareness expansion occurs during these moments of clarity.

I AM TAKING THE TIME
TO BE STILL AND SMELL
WHATEVER THE AIR BRINGS WITH IT.

6. SAVOR THE VARIETY OF LIFE

Our sense of taste is truly a blessing. After all...

VARIETY IS THE SPICE OF LIFE

We have receptors in our taste buds that react chemically with molecules that are mixed with our saliva. We have between 2000-5000 taste buds on our tongues, and other taste buds on the sides, roof, and in our throats. Each taste bud has between 50-100 receptor cells.

We have five categories of flavor, sweet, salty, sour, bitter, and savory.

Sweet, bitter, and savory flavors occur when a G-protein coupled receptor on the cell membrane combines with molecules. Saltiness is perceived when alkali metal enters the taste bud. When hydrogen atoms are absorbed, we experience sourness.

So we can describe the process of how we taste food from a standpoint of chemical reactions, receptors of information, and how our brains interpret the data and respond by causing other processes to occur including the release of endorphins, mastication, propulsion, digestion, absorption, transference of energy, and defecation. But why do we need to taste our food in the first place? The answer is simple...the process of nutrition can be enjoyable.

We are gifted with all of our Earthly Senses. These Senses can be described in terms of our physical reality through the various systems of biological processes that occur in our bodies, but are Spiritual. This Spiritual aspect cannot be observed, as it is immeasurable, but it can be experienced because the Spirit is felt.

As for our Sense of Taste, we have what seems like a small group of different types of flavors. What is interesting is that we employ all of our other Early Senses of Smell, Sight, Sound, Touch, Motion, Space, and Time through this process of consuming food and drinking liquids. We are well aware of how our Sense of Smell works in conjunction with Tasting food, but we sometimes forget how our Sense of Touch interprets texture. We are mostly not aware of how our ability to move our limbs through Space to take a fork or spoon to capture the morsel and place it in our mouth without expending any mental energy is a true blessing. If you ever become unable to feed yourself, which is a basic activity of daily living (ADL), you will realize how much of a gift our Sense of Space and Motion truly is. Even our ability to hear the process of pouring wine into a glass or the mastication of the food we are chewing has a soothing effect.

As for our Sense of Time... we often are barely conscious of it as we are unaware of how precious this form of currency is. Everything we feel is occurring through Time or we would not be aware of the experience ever happening to us. We would have no memory of our existence without Time.

The Sense of Taste is special because, although nutrition is necessary to sustain life, the variety of flavors is the icing on the proverbial cake. Theoretically, we do not need flavor at all as we have the urge to consume food, called hunger. Our overall satisfied feeling after we eat is caused by the digestion process of absorption beginning. If we are hungry enough, we will eat food, even if it does not taste good to us. I don't eat mollusks, mostly because of the slimy texture making me nauseous. The flavor is not enticing enough for me to typically eat anything from the mollusk phylum, but I would most certainly eat them if I was hungry enough.

Our Sense of Taste is a fun way to enjoy the necessary process of food and water consumption. We need to consume a certain amount of calories and water each day but have no limits to the variety of ways that we can enjoy these processes. Chefs are true artists, as they create intricate and beautifully complex mixtures of textures and flavors.

I APPRECIATE THE VARIETY OF LIFE.

7. A TOUCHING MOMENT

Our Sense of Touch is perhaps the most stimulating. We can feel everything physically through our largest organ, which is our skin. Our sense of touch is called the somatosensory system. This system is directly related to the nervous system and is composed of intricate interactions between sensory neurons and neural pathways. Sensory receptors exist all over the body in our skin, muscle tissue, tendons, ligaments, organs, and respiratory system. These neurons respond to stimuli outside and inside our bodies. The messages of information travel along nerve fibers and tell our limbs where to move and how to react.

Different types of receptors respond to their form of information. Thermoreceptors responding to changes in temperature are called nociception. This information is sent to mechanoreceptors, which tell muscle tissue how much contraction is necessary so that our Sense of Space (Proprioception) is also employed, which directs different combinations of movements with specific degrees of force to direct our limbs to the exact position that they need to be to conduct their next specific function.

When you grab a hot plate, for example, you do not have to think about the complex mathematical equations that describe the various angles of direction, and degrees of force needed to release the pressure necessary to let go of the plate. The split second necessary to perform the numerous calculations is done automatically and the reaction to the stimuli results in the action of letting go of the plate is performed.

Chemoreceptors work with the information that is provided through the stimuli that cause chemical reactions to occur, such as the release of endorphins that allow us to feel pleasure as well as the release of adrenaline, which gives us a burst of energy that enable us to conduct our fight or flight response.

The technical and chemical explanations of how we use our Sense of Touch to our benefit are complex but can be reduced to being described as a system of interactions between our cells and external stimuli, which is the absorption of information we know as Energy. These thousands of interactions that occur simultaneously for a partial second to maybe only a few seconds to a few minutes are conversations that are happening.

These touching moments are stored as memories. Some of the memories are fond ones, and others have left physical or emotional scars. All memories are readily accessible. Whenever we are feeling other than peaceful, we can easily access the fond memories and enjoy the same feelings that occurred when this moment was experienced for the first time.

The memories that are of the not-so-fond classification can be replayed just as easily. If we choose to relive those types of memories and re-experience them from a perspective of pain, we are giving ourselves another opportunity to learn the lesson. Upon the acceptance of truth as to why those painful experiences occurred in the first place, we will have absolved ourselves by resolving that particular riddle. Upon this allowance of full immersion of information to occur, we reveal another layer of discovery about who and what we are, which clears the way for our better understanding of why we are here on Earth currently. Upon the reconciliation of any past troubling, disturbing, or burdensome experiences, the Consciously Creative Being will happily use all reclassify those previously painful experiences as teachable moments for any who are still suffering because of their current perception of their experiences.

Our Sense of Touch is simply magical. We all have our Touching Moments. These experiences that occurred, are occurring, and will continue to occur on Earth offer the greatest range of variety from the pleasure and pain scale. The reality of our physical existence is understood by all living organisms from the single-celled life forms to the most illuminated of Human Beings. Our perception of the physical realm affects all three States of Conscious Being... Physical, Mental, and Emotional, and will allow us to become more aware of our other States of Spirituality.

Through our Sense of Touch, we can experience the worst kind of physical pain through to the most blissful states of pleasure. Every Touching Moment is intended to better inform us so that we may become more aware of our actual purpose as Human Beings.

Even if we do not become aware of this purpose, we are serving that purpose by simply existing. Our understanding of our role serves our Consciousness by increasing its rate of frequency and therefore increasing its power as well.

With this increase in power comes more knowledge, by which we can further expand our Awareness if we so choose. The expansion of our Awareness allows us to feel more of all aspects of our Consciousness, which brings forth more understanding and innerstanding. If we allow our feelings to expand freely, we realize that we can achieve anything that we wish. We will reach a point in our existence in which we believe that one beautiful premise…

ANYTHING IS POSSIBLE

8. PERCEPTUAL PROCESSING

Electromagnetic Radiation is an illusion. The reason EM Radiation is an illusion is that any given being is designed to process only a determined amount of data. All Beings that exist in the Physical Realm are subject to a limited perception of Reality. Human Beings can only see a limited range of the electromagnetic spectrum we know as visible light.

Every Being can process an amount of Energy equal to the mass of their physical body. Since $E=mc^2$, the balance of energy vs. matter is always currently being maintained. When you pass from the Physical Realm to the Spiritual Realm, your ability to see more of the Electro-magnetic Spectrum naturally increases.

The function of science is to better understand how various forms of Energy behaves so that we can better understand the known Universe. The concept of numbers seems to be inherent. Measuring is the most logical form of analysis. The use of symbols to depict the concepts is a creative invention of analysis.

Our ability to review images is based on the number of memory imprints that we have stored. This is how we process that data. We determine what we wish to process before experiencing each occurrence in our lives.

Every single bit of data that we process is first created in every conscious perception.

The dichotomies that become apparent are the basic form of analysis we call contrast. Yin/Yang describes this function and explains why there has to be One or the Other. One cannot come into existence without the Other. One needs the Other to become a union of Energy and Spirit. This communication is a Holy Communion in which Omega becomes an Alpha. The result is an occurrence in which a being experiences a Physical Reality.

Each of the 108 billion different human experiences occurred within a unique Consciousness. Every single second of each of those perceptual experiences occurred and is equally valid. For The Universe to process the amount of Energy it possesses, every living organism exists to serve the same purpose. The Universe is experiencing itself through every living Perceptual Processor.

We can alter our beliefs to accept that all living beings serve the same purpose. Is it a stretch to believe that everything in The Universe serves the same purpose as well? Once we acknowledge that every single particle is part of a Grand Design, we can take the next step by concluding that every bit of matter that ever existed is consciously connected.

This connection is described in the scientific field of study of physics as Quantum Entanglement. The Law of One is the Spiritual explanation of the same phenomenon. If every piece of Energy is serving the One and the Other, each bit is potentially illuminating.

The moment we are being prejudicial about experiencing any occurrence, we determine our fate. We are telling the Universe that we wish to not communicate with that Energy. We are going to remain as aware as we were at the beginning of the communication. No being is entirely ignorant. We are all unaware of certain pieces of knowledge.

Every Being is born innocent. Every Being is meant to experience every single occurrence that happens to them. The moment the Sentient Being has the Realization that every occurrence is a learning experience, the moment they take conscious and creative control over their destiny. They are no longer going to wallow in darkness. Consciously aware Beings are either being peaceful or becoming peaceful.

9. ENJOY THE RIDE

Life is simply a process in which we have a physical body, a mind, and emotions through which receive information. We absorb, transform, and use that data to allow our Consciousness to perceive our Reality however we wish to expand our Awareness. Free Will allows us to believe whatever we wish and either take experiences as they come and be a responsible being or a consciously creative being. Whether you consciously choose the thoughts that you can use as a foundation to design your vision of Reality or respond to what life offers you, the ability of Perceptual Processing is ever-present.

Whether you come from a perspective of determining the reality of your existence or having the mystical experience of Maya forming the actual nature of your life, you always can either have fun with the learning processes of life or not. For some, being angry and confused is an enjoyable experience or they would grow tired of that method of obtaining information and divert from that path.

As a kid, I truly loved the ups and downs of the roller coaster. I learned so much through my life experiences. I have been blessed with such a wide range of Frequencies. I have experienced Everything from the darkness, silence, and stillness of The None to the lightness, music, and motion of The One. Even within the Physical Realm, I have felt various degrees of pain through the scale to blissful pleasure. Mentally, I have experienced depression, obsessive-compulsive disorder, attention deficit disorder, drug addiction, psychotic breakdowns, utter confusion, and various degrees of lucidity. Emotionally, I have felt worry, doubt, fear, hatred, disgust, envy, pride, respect, appreciation, happiness, supreme joy, and peaceful serenity. The wild ride on the roller coaster was truly an amazing adventure.

Over time and having experienced enough contrasts, I found that I enjoy an even and peaceful merry-go-round type of ride. The way for me to be free is to simply appreciate everything that occurs without exception. It's easy to be grateful for the experiences that feel good, but not an easy task to have at least a respectful degree of appreciation for those really painful experiences. Instead of complaining about anything, revel in those experiences that are the most painful. Remember the last time you smashed your elbow? Did you wallow in misery or did you chuckle to yourself or maybe even let out a laughing ouch or yell some profane words? You realized immediately that the pain hurt like hell but was not going to last forever. That is the funniest thing about pain...it only lasts long enough for us to accept the truth in whatever lesson is being taught to us. Each lesson we learn reveals another layer of truth about ourselves and with each discovery, we become less confused and believe in ourselves more. As our beliefs grow, we better understand why we are here.

Upon the Revelation of our true purpose, everything becomes more clear. We know what needs to be done because we realize that every thought causes emotions that drive our will to either take actions that will further propel our vision. These actions move our vision from existing in dream form into a state in which any new information will mold the images of that vision toward the manifested state of being our Reality.

So enjoy the entire adventure, including the ride to the amusement park, standing in line, and chit-chatting with your loved ones waiting for the rollercoaster, eating the cotton candy, going on the merry-go-round, and driving home exhausted but happy after spending the day laughing and having fun.

Your life is an adventure. Enjoy the ride whether you are off-roading and it's bumpy as hell, or fast and smooth. As you become aware enough to know deep within your heart that your life matters and what you do in life affects everyone within earshot of you if you are speaking, six feet of you if you are strongly vibrating any frequency, or line-of-sight if you are moving with a purpose. Yes, every motion you take, the emotion you feel, and the thoughts that cross your mind matter, and can make all of the difference in the World.

Pay attention to your Spirit Level by listening to your feelings. The Spirit is easily affected. Whenever you feel off-kilter or out of balance, The Spirit can be drained. Recognizing when this is occurring will allow you to refill The Spirit by being kind and freely giving your time to the next being that is drawn to you.

10. BEING PEACEFUL OR BECOMING PEACEFUL

Diverging from oppositional dichotomies such as Positive/Negative, Good/Bad, Right/Wrong, True/False, even Go/Stop, and On/Off has been very useful. By doing so, I have been sufficiently allowing my Consciousness to accept more amounts of information than I had previously.

By being more aware of waves of peacefulness, I have become more peaceful than ever before. By simply paying attention to how I feel, I have been able to recognize friction before it turns into a severe irritants or anything truly painful. Do I still feel annoyed, frustrated, or confused at times? Yes, I do.

During moments of Conscious Awareness of the Momentary Present (CAMP), I would ask myself if I felt Peaceful or Other Than Peaceful (OTP). If I felt Peaceful, I would continue doing whatever it was that I was doing so that I could maintain that Sound Frequency. If I was OTP, I would choose an activity that I believed would create new peacefulness.

This was working fine until I realized that by judging feelings as OTP, I was causing those feelings to affect my Well Being. I was allowing myself to feel however I believed I deserved how to feel. I was not suffering at all, but I was testing myself. I have concluded that my ability to be hyper-aware of how I feel will provide even more opportunities to present themselves at even faster rates of frequency.

I realized that I do not need to try to know anything more than I currently know. That does not mean that I am not curious or that I believe that I know it all. I had the Realization months ago that I know only one thing…

HOW I FEEL NOW

I also realized that I do not need to ever try to do anything ever again. Everything that we *Try* to do is because we think we are lacking in something. We believe that we need material things or large amounts of money. We believe that we need to have the approval of others. We never needed anyone's approval. We only need their love.

I had perhaps the most significant Revelation recently about Being Peaceful. I became aware that I can feel however I wish about anything I choose. This may sound like a simple notion. It sounds simple because it is as simple as can be. We allow ourselves to feel however we believe we deserve to feel. If you believe that God Loves you unconditionally and without exception, imagine how you will find yourself feeling most of the time.

I now re-remember that I am always either One or the Other. I am Being Peaceful when I am present. I am Being Peaceful when I am appreciating my family and friends. I am Being Peaceful when I am playing my guitar. I am Being Peaceful when I speak about or write about philosophy.

There are times when, instead of Being Peaceful, I am Becoming Peaceful. It is understandable to think otherwise. I do, however, find it more of an even transition to go from Becoming Peaceful to Being Peaceful. Many enjoy a more extreme roller coaster style of ride that is smooth but has high peaks and low valleys.

I appreciate Peacefulness. I find myself being more productive during these Serene States of mind. Finding a balance between my Mental, Physical, and Emotional States of Being is where that Zero Point Energy is most easily felt.

I AM ALWAYS
BEING PEACEFUL OR
BECOMING PEACEFUL

11. BEING PERFECTLY STILL

What is the one thing we have an infinite supply of, that exists in Space (of which there is an unlimited amount), can be perceived as being present, and can be consciously altered?

TIME

Without Time, we have no When for anything to occur. Everything requires time to be or it cannot exist. The most accurate depictions of this phenomenon have to do with the dimension of motion. All Things appear to move in some fashion or another. Things are perceived to be spinning, rotating, vibrating, or traveling from one point to another. All movement achieves one thing...a change in position in the Space-Time Continuum. Every form of measurement has the element of motion. Motion is the change of a particle or piece of a waveform. That change is a modulation of where it is positioned in the Universe and the duration of time that it takes to make that change.

There is an ongoing debate about whether Time exists at all or if it is another illusion of Reality. To deny anything exists is understandable, but unreasonable. Anything that you conceive can exist, as anything is possible. Time must exist in some fashion or we would not be discussing it. The argument is whether Linear Time exists or if it is only a figment of our imagination. I contend that it is both. Linear Time exists or nothing would occur to us. If Energy is information, and we were capable of understanding everything all at once, we would not need Time to exist. We would not need to exist, because we would already know everything. Everything that occurs to us is because of our ability to decode pieces of data over periods. This ability to decipher information is achieved through one of the functions of Consciousness called Perception.

I believe that we can agree that Time has many aspects and ways to be viewed and understood. Time's true essence is that it is infinite. There is an unlimited duration of Time because there is an immeasurable amount of Space. We have Infinity, which is the limitless When and Where Reality can, does, and will continue to occur.

That conjunction of Time & Space is the Zero Point of Infinity $\{0 \cdot (\infty)\}$. In this Splace, our position is devoid of Electromagnetic-Energy, is dead silent, and perfectly still. The degree of peacefulness in this Eternal Here and Now is beyond measure.

All Electro-magnetic Energy radiates, which simply means it oscillates or is described as vibrating. The absence of Electromagnetic Radiation is an aspect of Dark Matter, which is Pure Spirit. Without EM Radiation, we have no flow of information. This information serves only to further develop Consciousness by increasing its rate of frequency. Each Consciousness is part of the Collective Consciousness and is continually receiving and transmitting Energy. Our brains are Transceivers through which interactive communications are continuously occurring whether we are aware of these interactions or not. At some point, our curiosity is satisfied and we can remain in stasis by simply Oscillating at a rate that has minimal to zero fluctuation.

"The Sound of Silence" by Simon and Garfunkel is one of my favorite songs of all time. What does silence sound like? It is not heard, but it is felt. Our Heart Space is where the Sound is felt. We are gifted with our Sense of Sound and can appreciate the sounds of nature or the sound of music. When would we appreciate the silence of the Sound? I contend that when we only require the healing nature of Being Sound when something needs to change its form. If we desire no change, we are therefore content to be silent.

There is indescribable Peace within this period in which Sound is unmoving. This space is the duration in between the crest and the trough…it is the Zero Point position where Time is not felt. This is where Time is seemingly lost. Everything becomes apparent in this Present Moment.

To be silent is to be free of the motion of Sound Waves. This state of being is Stillness. When the Sentient Being is currently well informed with Energy, and content being Peacefully Sound, there is where the need to move about or change position is unnecessary. This Stillness is the point in Time and space where nothing matters. This is when no things are currently necessary to change how you feel then. This is why Nothingness matters because it becomes necessary to become clear yet again.

There are beautiful reasons why one would wish to be perfectly still. There are many methods through which one can find themselves there. You are genetically engineered and designed to connect to The Universal Source in your special way. Your lifetime of experiences is the clue in which you may rediscover the secrets to simply Being Present by feeling Perfectly Still.

I encourage you to find your way and reveal how to Re-feel and Re-remember how you once were. I believe with all of my Heart that you will be pleasantly surprised that you already know all that you need to know to feel as Peaceful as you wish to feel. You never need to suffer ever again.

PART FIVE

OUR EARTHLY REALM

CHAPTER ONE

THE EIGHT PILLARS OF EXISTENCE

1. FROM SPACE TO SOUL

- ❖ Space
- ❖ Time
- ❖ Gravity
- ❖ Karma
- ❖ Consciousness
- ❖ Awareness
- ❖ Spirit
- ❖ Soul

(Space) - Where

All things require a place to be. Anyplace can become Anywhere. Without a Where, nothing can come into existence. Wherever something has an infinite amount of space to exist, the potential for that thing to become Anything, and have no limits to its size or scope of existence becomes a Reality.

Space is neither seen, heard, nor even felt. We can only sense things as they come into existence upon their arrival in Space from the Elsewhere.

(Time) - When

Without Time, there is no When for any occurrence to take place. Although linear Time is an Illusion, that does not mean it does not exist in your Reality.

Time can be measured in increments of designated duration, but Time itself is neither seen nor heard. The effects of Time are seen and felt.

Time becomes less relevant the more attention you pay to the only thing that matters. The only thing that ever truly mattered is the Eternal Now.

(Gravity) - What

Scientists see what Gravity does, but cannot see Gravity waves or particles. We Feel the effects of Gravity every moment of our lives but never hear its sound.

Gravity is an expression of The Law of One. It seems that Everything is already connected to The One. All Things have always been connected to every other one. We are All One through the Soul. We Are WON NOW.

(Karma) - How

Karma is the fair, just, and effective Energy Prosecutor. The Law of Karma is that you determine your fate by judging yourself. If you think you can get away with causing another Being harm without feeling ALL of the Energy that you created, think again. That Energy includes any that the Being you intentionally harmed perpetuated by re-enacting the experience that caused them trauma.

You can gauge the level of Karmic Energy required to be processed by how much Fear you feel. There are a lot of various Emotions and Feelings, but...Fear sums up the best description of the indicator of the most important lesson based on When it should be addressed. When you face that which you fear the most first, all other Fear-based lessons will naturally come quite easily. Your Faith will grow exponentially as it seems to have an inverse relationship to Fear. That which we Fear the most requires an equivalent level of Faith to Overcome.

When you pay close attention to your Feelings by simply allowing them to flow without any barriers in your Belief System, you will Become more conscious of Who you are while Being aware of What you are Becoming. With these Realizations and Revelations, you Become more knowledgeable about Why you are here.

(Consciousness) - Who

Who are you? Before you ask any other questions, you are compelled to address this one pressing question. Until you resolve the riddle, you feel confused, angry, lonely, and afraid.

Upon acceptance of Who you are, you become aware of how your Consciousness works. You become more creative. You become more perceptive. You become more willing to communicate how awesomely Peaceful you are currently Being.

(Awareness) - What

Once you accept all aspects of Who you are, even if you do not fully understand some of your gifts, skills, or attributes, you begin to wonder

What you are. You are What you Feel. Whatever it is that you Feel that you are, is exactly What you are.

If you don't believe in yourself, how can you possibly Become What you are meant to Become? Listen to how you Feel. Do not trust anything or anyone other than yourself when it comes to your level of Faith.

You are Whatever you believe you are and can achieve Whatever you wish. Anything is possible.

(Spirit) - Way

We enjoy rediscovering knowledge that we have already learned. We have these Realizations and Revelations that lift our Spirits. Whenever we accept the truth in anything, our Oscillating Rate of Conscious Frequency increases. Whenever we allow ourselves to Feel however we happen to Feel, our Awareness expands.

Our Spirits guide us through the whole life experience. The Spirits are our Feelings. We can always trust our Feelings as we know that the source is The One. Our SPIRitsinSPIRe us.

This Is The Way.

(Soul) - Why

The Soul is Ours to be One with All. One for All and Won for Now.

The Soul is God Being with us, living through us, and because of us so that he may live for us.

God Becomes more knowledgeable by Becoming more conscious through us. God is Being as aware as we allow ourselves to Be.

God is always present here and now. If you are still and pay attention to your Consciousness, you will know God is there. If you are silent and listen to your Feelings, you will be aware of how Peaceful you can always Be.

These 8 Pillars are God's Gifts to you. You may do whatever you wish with these Blessings. You may create anything that you desire. All things are possible through God. There is only infinite potential waiting for you.

BE AS PEACEFUL AS YOU WISH TO BE. HAVE FAITH THAT
GOD LOVES YOU. ALLOW YOURSELF TO BECOME WHAT YOU
ARE MEANT TO BE.
JUST BE YOURSELF. EXPRESS YOURSELF.
ENJOY THE PROCESS.

2. A SP(L)ACE IN TIME

What is Space? Space is the Where. We can begin understanding Anything by knowing what it is not. Space is not seen. Space is not heard. Space is not felt. Space is not measurable. Space is not Anything other than a Where.

Space is (S)omewhere
Space is (E)verywhere.
Space is (E)ternal.
Space is (N)owhere.

These effects of Space are SEEN, but Absolute Space only possesses Energetic Frequencies that are seen.

Space is…

Spacious
Enveloping
Allowing
Liberating

Space is certainty Something. It has unlimited room for Anything and Everything to occur. Space is misunderstood by many as being the 3rd Dimension.

A dimension is an aspect of an existing object that can be measured. Anything that can be measured, must be observed via Electro-magnetic Energy.

Dimensions are traditionally understood as divisions of Reality. We have been taught that our physical existence relies on Dimensions 1-4.

One can create a formation that has 3 Dimensions, such as a ⬚. This item is not the 3rd Dimension. An actual Cube has 3 Dimensions that can be described as length, width, and height. The size of the Cube can be measured, as well as its weight. If the Cube is empty, it would have a measurable volume. A perfect vacuum can exist, as *Anything Is Possible*, but is not very probable. There would have to be an impenetrable exterior for atoms to not be able to escape. The only surface that would not allow for anything to escape would have to be perfectly solid. In other words, there would be no movement of any subatomic particles and so dense that not even light could escape. This Cube would have to become a black hole, at which time our thought experiment falls apart. Since Space is infinite, and cannot be measured, it is therefore immeasurable. Space is then not the 3rd Dimension in and of itself.

Space is The Zeroth Dimension. Space is the place of origin. Space is the Omega for the creation of Anything. A place in Space Becomes a Thing that has the potential to Be Anything and go Anywhere else it wishes to be. Space is Where Anything would be able to last Forever because Space is infinite. Space is the one thing that Everything has in common.

Space is a Something.

Space is in Everything.

Space is within Nothing.

Space is a Splace where Time means Nothing while remaining a Place in Reality in which Time does matter and makes a difference.

Space is all we need to begin to exist.

SPACE IS THE PLACE TO BE AND THE ONLY SPLACE WE WILL EVER TRULY NEED.

3. TIME ETERNAL

What is Time?

As with all things...begin by contemplating what Time is not. Time is not seen, but you can observe the passage of Time as it relates to the motion of other objects. Time is not felt, but you can have a sense of its passage. Time is not heard. It makes no Sound, but you can hear the division of Linear Time. The Space in between the Sonic Occurrences can be measured in increments.

Time is not the 4th Dimension as we have believed. Time is not a Dimension at all, but is dimensional, as it can be measured linearly. Being infinite, Time cannot be wasted. Time's perfect state of Being is expressed as Eternity. If Anything could be Anywhere, while Being there however long it wanted to Be, then Anything would have sufficient time to achieve whatever it wanted. They would have all of the Time in the World.

So What can Time be?

Time is Infinite.

Time is an expression of Life.

Time is the interval between two occurrences.

Time is an Illusion.

Time is expressed through the force of Friction. Time allows a Being to experience an occurrence. The Awareness of the occurrence is always felt in the present MOMent. Even if your Consciousness is somewhere other than Now, your Awareness is always Present. When you are reliving the past, if you Feel Peaceful by fondly reminiscing without expectations of how long the experience will last, you Become aware of Being Present. When you live in the past, but Feel shame, regret, or remorse, your Consciousness is still actually in the Present Moment. In your Reality, your Awareness is only reFEELing the past because you have yet to stop punishing yourself. These Revelations are profound.

If you live with Hope for a brighter future and do so with Faith, your level of Belief is maintained through your Consciousness while your Awareness verifies this allowance of Energy to occur through how Peaceful you feel in that NOW. If you live in Fear of your future by placing an assumption that something is going to Feel horrible, then you determine your destiny by drawing more of that Frequency of Energy toward you. This will extend the feeling because you are creating a more painful experience.

Your Reality is based on how you perceive the passage of Time to be going. Without Time, the opportunity to experience any event never happens because it cannot occur without friction. The force of Friction causes the Frequency Currents to change their motion. The transformation of Energy from one State of Being to another forces the information to become absorbed through heat induction.

Time is an Illusion and yet a necessary part of Reality. Time allows any Being the ability to absorb data through all of the Senses. Without one's Sense of Time, paying attention to the data becomes less necessary. During these present moments, one simply goes from Becoming more Conscious to Being more Aware.

One can Recognize when they should pay closer attention consciously because there is a direct relationship between the level of Friction and the importance of the data during the DURation of Time of these occurrences. This is why we talk about enduring pain. Hear the similarity between *Paying Attention & Pain Attention?*

When we ignore the pain, we are disregarding the SIGNs, SIGNals, and SIGNifiers. By doing so, we are not paying attention to that which is SIGNificant. We can mask the pain, but the issue will persist and fester. This is how we become sick and diseased. All ILLnesses are an ILLusion, but very painful, irritating, disruptive, or disturbing.

Time causes Friction. The effects can be painful. All issues can be addressed. All problems have solutions. All questions have answers. All Energy can be reprocessed to become useful information.

All we need to do to spend our Time Wisely is to simply Pay Attention to the Present Moment. If an Illusion gains our attention, and we Feel Peaceful, allow ourselves to simply Be Sound. If we feel any level of Friction and we recognize what is occurring to us, we can start the learning process immediately. If we view pain as only a Sign, which is a form of communication, then we get to work processing the information. If we view pain as a form of punishment, we will either decide that we do not wish to be punished and disregard the data or we will perceive Time to slow down. We will suffer needlessly. If we pay closer attention, Time will speed back up as we process the data. When we become hyper-focused, Time becomes irrelevant and Feels almost perfectly still. We will Feel more Peaceful.

The Realizations and Revelations of how to use Time to your advantage hinge on your Belief System. If you believe that you deserve to be punished, then you will determine your amount of suffering. If you believe that God Truly Loves you, then you will be more patient with your Life Processing.

I Believe God Loves All.
I Believe God Is Merciful.
I Believe In God.

I AM BEING WHO
I AM SO THAT
I WILL BECOME WHO
I AM MEANT TO BE

WHO ARE YOU BEING?

4. GRAVITY'S DENSITY DESTINY

Gravity is not a Force. It is a FIELD.

(F)eeling
(I)nfinite
(E)nergy
(L)essens
(D)ensity

Gravity, like Space and Time, is neither Seen nor Heard. We do Sense Gravity. The effects of Gravity are felt through our Sense of Balance in our Physical Body.

Gravity seems to express itself through motion. It doesn't increase the Frequency of Energy, but only the intensity of how it feels. Gravity is directly related to Time and Space but is not forcing itself upon any other object or particle.

The effects of Gravity are seen, but Gravity itself is invisible. Gravity is a Field because it reveals itself through your sense of Motion. Gravity is akin to Time and Space, as it is neither seen nor heard.

Gravity is Felt.
Gravity is Attraction.

Gravity is Invisible.
Gravity is useful in determining where our attention can best be spent.

Quantum Entanglement verifies what we already know and are learning to accept as the Truth. It shows us that all things are already connected. Gravity is an expression of Gaia that we feel through our Bodies. Our Reality is determined by How we feel. Through Gravity, we determine how much density we will feel. What we are feeling is Gravity. We create our Destiny by the thoughts that we choose. What we are is Our Awareness. How we are is based on What we feel. We deserve to feel however we choose to perceive all information that is processed through our Mental, Physical, and Emotional Bodies.

As you become more aware of how you feel, your Awareness will naturally expand through the processing of Energy through the expression of Gravity. The less conscious of your Awareness you happen to Be, the denser you will Feel.

As you become more aware, the Space that you occupy becomes less dense. Your Consciousness has a conversation with the Awareness and as more truthful information is utilized, your Consciousness Becomes more powerful.

This power creates a clear path through any material (anything that matters). This clarity is also known as Lucidity.

As you become more Lucid, you are Illuminated. Your Spirits will rise in direct correlation with your Life Force Energy. The effects of Gravity will seem to be less noticeable. When you feel more powerful, you have more confidence. When you are confident, you believe in yourself. You have Faith that your Vision will come into Being. Dreams Become Reality.

Orville and Wilbur Wright experienced the process of Enlightenment from 1901-1903. Their historic flight at Kitty Hawk on December 17, 1903, literally defied Gravity.

There were several milestones in aeronautics. One of my favorites was achieved by Brigadier General Charles Elwood Yeager. On October 14, 1947, Chuck Yeager broke the Sound Barrier. He went Mach 1 at an altitude of 45,000 Feet (8.5 miles). Orville Wright was alive to hear about this achievement.

The Soviet Union was the first Country to achieve departure from Earth's Atmosphere. On April 12, 1961, Soviet Cosmonaut Yuri Gagarin became the first person in Space when he orbited the Earth in a Vostock spacecraft.

All of these events proved that we are not bound by the force of Gravity. We are only tethered by our Level of Consciousness. We impose our limits on what we can achieve through our Belief System. Through our determination and Will, we persevere and overcome all obstacles. We decide that we want to do something and imagine what it will look and feel like. We absorb all information that pertains to the creation of that Vision and process the user data.

Gravity is Field Guide. Trust your Feelings. Use all of your Senses to use all information to develop every aspect of your Being.

An increased amount of Density of matter (Physical Body) will slow your movement. If you feel tired physically, pay attention to your Body. What are you putting into your body? I grew up in Glendora, California, USA. My hometown was famous for being the smoggiest town in Los Angeles County. We had smog alerts. A Red Stage meant we could not go outside for recess. During these smoggy days, your lungs hurt with deep breaths. If you do not take in sufficient amounts of air, your ability to exert yourself becomes limited. The density of the air is greater with the accumulation of pollutants. Your Frequency is affected by what nutrients you consume. Pay attention to anything that goes into your body whether through Respiration, Ingestion, and Hydration. Be very cautious with any type of Injection.

Our Mental State of Being is also affected by Gravity.

More Density of things that don't matter (Mental State) will cloud your vision, causing you to feel anxious or fearful. If you accept deceitful thoughts or concepts into your Consciousness, your stress levels will rise. Your nervous system will react by resonating with those dense thought forms.

"We Create Our Destiny By The Thoughts That We Choose."
-Michael Wilson Evrard

More Density of the only things that matter (Emotions) will cause confusion, anger, and frustration. We get confused when we receive mixed signals. When another Being is unclear when they think, speak, or act, then any who is within their toroidal field will not know how to read them. If the recipient of the information assumes that the one delivering the message is intending on deceiving or causing them harm, then a potential conflict will develop.

Each Communication Participant is responsible for whatever occurs next.

Gravity affects all 3 Earthly States of Being…Physical, Mental, and Emotional.

Each Conscious Being is responsible for their Spiritual Development. Because of Free Will, each Soul Being must choose their path. The only allowance made by God is that of Light or Sound Bearers freely expressing themselves as per their Free Will Contract.

I AM FREELY CHOOSING
MY THOUGHT FREQUENCIES

5. KARMIC CLEANSING

Who is Karma and how does she work? Karma is an expression of Divine Feminine Energy. She is not a bitch. Please show some respect. Karma is not a form of punishment. Karma does not smite, torment, torture, or cause any form of pain. Each Being creates their Reality however they see fit. Time causes Friction as a means to signal a Being to pay attention. Karma never means any harm.

Karma is perfectly Fair.
Karma is always Giving.
Karma is Compassionate.
Karma is Merciful.

Karma blesses us with a system through which we may be cleansed. If we only did one thing with The Golden Rule in mind...

DO UNTO OTHERS
AS YOU WOULD
HAVE THEM
DO UNTO YOU

That one thing is very simple and it is this...

LOVE ONE ANOTHER

There is no way to misinterpret this if you apply The Golden Rule. If your concept of Love is skewed, and you discourage another from expressing themselves, then Karma will show you exactly what you are doing. For example...if your intentions are "good" or "well-meaning," but you are dictating how you think another should act, then you are violating the Law of One. Whenever you impose your Will on others, whether or not you have good intentions, you are draining their Spirits.

This is tantamount to Spiritual Bullying. You are trying to determine their fate.

Now...these types of actions, especially when well-intended, are not sinful. They do, however, require additional guidance. Karma is perfectly fair, balanced, and reasonable when providing Energy in direct proportion to that which is given. An act that is disparaging or discouraging can be disheartening to the one receiving that Energy, but they are responsible for their own Karma.

The intentions of the one communicating or giving their Energy dictate the degree of return on their investment. If they intend to cause harm, then the recipient of that Energy will read it as such and they will experience whatever level of Energy they perceive it to be. The return of that intentional Energy will come back with an equivalent amount of that type of Energy that was originally generated by that Being. That payback would include any extraneous Energy that was passed along by the initial recipient. Each Being is responsible for their own Karma, however. If the recipient of the initial offering of Energy re-enacts an experience to make sense of what occurred to them, then they are not intentionally harming another. The instigator of that Energetic Cycle is the one who receives ALL of it back.

Karma is the Effect of Causality. One who believes that they are not bound by Karmic Energy is in for a ride. I was going to use the term *rude awakening,* but that is disrespectful to Karma. When we feel guilty about something, we really should pay attention. Our Feelings are communicating deep messages to us. All that we have to do is be still and listen.

When you disregard any Feelings or refute the validity of any signals, you are only procrastinating. You always know deep down when you are doing something that impedes another's journey. Anytime you dampen the Spirit of another, you are only adding to the rockiness of your own. These obstacles increase with your level of arrogance.

Each Being is way more powerful than they can imagine during the early stages of their development.

Ones who are *Hell Bent* on intentionally causing harm are very conscious of their power. They are quite unaware of the effects those destructive actions will have on their Spirits. Think about it...if they only knew how Karma operates. I say "operates" because Karma is very precise in her Spiritual Operations. She is a Spiritual Surgeon.

Karma knows when to time her surgery. Many choose to create what they think is paradise on Earth. A Hedonistic Being is only creating their version of Hell in the Spirit Realm.

God knows what we need. God also allows us to choose what we want to experience. Since God Loves All with NO EXCEPTIONS, no being is capable of doing Anything that would make God do anything but continue to Love that Being. That does not mean Causality does not come into play.

Time Causes Everything to occur through the Force of Friction, which increases your Oscillating Rate of Conscious Frequency, making that being more conscious.

Karma is Effective in Allowing a Willing Being to become more aware of how they feel.

What you choose to do with your increased power and wisdom is up to your Free Will.

The best part of this process called LIFE is that the only limits are always self-imposed. We generate resistance by what causes us to live in fear. We can allow Karma to cleanse the way after Time clears the path to become more lucid.

All of what we experience occurs in our Imagination. These images, visions, thoughts, and ideas are all Frequencies that will resonate with however we are Feeling.

Some believe that they can have all of their Karmic Debt paid in full. This Belief allows one to proceed thinking that their journey will be smooth sailing. Depending on the power of that particular Consciousness, then yes...they have determined their fate. They are satisfied with how Peaceful they feel. Others wish to go deeper with the Revelation that Karma is on call for Eternity.

If you wish to experience God's Will, allow Karma to proceed with her role. There is always more to learn. Karma will always be there for you. There is no final destination for those who truly wish for God's Will to be done for them.

6. CREATIVE CONSCIOUSNESS

Consciousness is not what we think it is. Consciousness is not detectable. Consciousness is not measurable. Consciousness is not limited in its power. Consciousness is not located in our brains.

Consciousness is causal.
Consciousness is creative.
Consciousness is perceptive.
Consciousness is powerful.

Consciousness is the cause of thoughts, ideas, and most importantly, our Beliefs. Everything that one does is caused by its Consciousness. Our deepest desires originate from our Subconscious. We often wonder where our thoughts come from when they seem to just pop into our heads. Everything comes from Somewhere. The place of that Somewhere is known as the Subconscious Mind.

All experiences begin as a Thought Form. A Thought Form is a concept or idea that triggers an Emotion. We either react or respond to those emotions by creating scenarios in which we wish to experience an occurrence that we believe will allow us to Feel a certain way.

Consciousness is directly responsible for the creation of our Reality. We generate a vision of what we want to occur. The strength of our Belief

System will either propel our vision or dispel it. The Universe does not discern between what we think we want. The Universe does not communicate in thoughts or even Beliefs. The Universe speaks to all Beings in the language of Wave Form Frequencies. Your Consciousness will Oscillate at the rate that corresponds to the Feelings that are maintained by your Beliefs. Your Beliefs are strengthened by the images that you can hold in your Consciousness.

The part of your Consciousness that is responsible for generating these images is your Imagination. You design your vision as you wish to see it. If your Belief System is underdeveloped, you will not use your Energy to make the blueprints. Your ideas will be overrun by doubtful thoughts.

Everything your Consciousness does is based upon what you believe. Since you have an infinite amount of Space and an Eternity in which to accomplish your Dream, freeing your mind to be as elaborate as you wish only increases your chances of a successful Manifestation. Your perceptual lens in your Imagination will work more efficiently if your Perspective is always fresh and your Perception is not clouded with static dust.

Your Perception is the key to efficiently using your Time and effectively using your Conscious Frequency. If your Perception is skewed in any manner, your Vision will not be attainable. The believability depends on its clarity. Something so hard to imagine is due to a Perspective that disallows you to be at an angle from which to see the light. The lack of clarity might be occurring because of an unclear field of view, that will remain unapparent as long as your Perception is not tuned into the frequencies that are being transmitted.

Your Consciousness is very powerful. Your Free Will allows you to alter your Consciousness in many different ways. The three primary functions of your Consciousness are...

1. Creation
2. Perception
3. Communication

All methods of operation of the Consciousness are dependent on your Belief System. You strengthen your Beliefs by consciously practicing all three functions.

Using your Imagination and Perception, you process information. Whenever you accept user data, your Oscillating Conscious Frequency increases its rate. This feeling is akin to being high. It is blissful and exhilarating.

Acceptance of all data is how you become more consciously knowledgeable. Knowledge is power, so with this influx of Information, what used to be a problem is no longer an issue. As you get better at solving your dilemmas, your mind becomes more lucid. With this increase in clarity, your Perception changes. With these alterations, your Imagination flourishes, and your Beliefs grow. As you further develop your Belief System, you Become more creative and confident.

With confidence comes courage. When you are feeling courageous, you are more willing to take on those things that you fear. Everything that you fear become a barrier. Those barriers debilitate your ability to believe in yourself. Whenever your Beliefs dwindle, your Spirits will be drained. Defend all aspects of your Being with a Free Spirit, a Compassionate Heart, and an Open Mind.

If you feel Other Than Peaceful, recognize those Feelings as the guides that they are. Learn whatever you can from all experiences and move on once you have reconciled all differences. Spend your time as wisely as possible by Being present for communications with Anyone who encourages you to believe in yourself. Interact with Anything that inspires you to express yourself freely. Whenever you learn how to overcome an obstacle, share that knowledge with others.

LOVE ONE ANOTHER
BE KIND TO YOURSELF

7. WHAT IS AWARENESS

What does it mean to be a Human Being? What you are is expressed in many ways. You possess a Physical Body, but that is not What you are. Your body is an Energy processing plant. It gathers Light and Sound Forms. You possess a Mind, but that is only there to process Thoughts. It acts as a filter. You also possess Emotions. You can Be happy, sad, angry, or however you wish to be, but your Emotions don't make you What you are.

What you are is how you Feel. Everything you think, do, say, or believe is based on how you feel. Every choice, decision, or emotion is created because of how you feel about it. You are not what you feel. You are aware of what you feel.

Your power is caused by your Consciousness. Your Awareness is the effect of how you Feel. If your Consciousness is Who you are, your Awareness is What you are because it is How you feel.

1=Consciousness
0=Awareness
1=Cause
0=Effect

1=Becoming
0=Being
1=Light
0=Sound

We can feel the effects of anything our Consciousness causes. We can Become more conscious of our Awareness while Being aware of our Consciousness. We can see Light Forms while Feeling Sound.

We can receive data in various ways through different Electro-magnetic Frequencies. We have new senses that we are Becoming more aware of, but are still learning how to process Energy from all of our Basic 5 Senses. We are re-remembering how to absorb information not just by what we See or Hear, but by what we Smell, Taste, and Touch as well.

Your Consciousness processes the information that is received through all of your Senses. When you accept this data without preconceived notions or prejudices, your brain will automatically filter through the information and absorb the most useful bits of data. This causes your bodily systems to work together and trigger a series of chemical reactions resulting in the release of a variety of endorphins. All of these events create an experience that allows your Awareness to engage in the interaction.

Your Awareness allows you to Feel every piece of information that you accept as potentially useful. When you prevent any data from coming into your Light Vessel, you are deciding that it is not meant for you. Upon the recognition of all light forms being useful, you will simply be allowing for more truth to illuminate your Consciousness, which will cause your Awareness to expand.

Anything that causes confusion, anxiety, distress, or misery will be indicative of you doing one thing: overthinking. All of these types of suffering become affixed to our Consciousness. They become attachments. They create a new desire, which in turn causes us to suffer more. Instead of wishing to no longer suffer, we can become more aware of the purpose of suffering.

What exactly is the purpose of suffering? This is one of the most significant questions of our existence as Human Beings. Regardless of our understanding of The Universe, I believe Humans all can connect in one way. Before we can fully understand Anything, we must have an understanding of ALL. What is *ALL?*

ALL is (A)nything.
ALL is (W)henever.
ALL is (E)verywhere.

Whenever we Become more aware of Anything, Whatever it may be, we better understand its purpose. When we better understand Something's purpose, we are more able to accept Why it exists. When we accept something's reason for Being, we will have Compassion for it. With Acceptance comes the Allowance of Becoming more aware. With Illumination comes Expansion of Awareness.

Whenever we Become more aware of any point in time we find ourselves, Whenever, that may be, we Realize that the only time that Ever Matters is The Present. At that moment of Awareness, then and only then are you going to Feel Whatever you are supposed to Feel to experience whatever it is you will reveal more Truth. This Allowance of Love is a Revelation.

Upon the Realization that Revelations occur Wherever you allow them to occur, you Wherever Becomes Anywhere and Everywhere.

Your Imagination will fire and ignite IDEAS.

(I)magination
(D)raws
(E)nergy
(A)nywhere
(S)patially

Our Belief System will grow with every Illuminated Monumental MOMent in which our Consciousness increases its rate of frequency (Realizations) or the expansion of Awareness (Revelations) through simply Being Sound.

These Realizations and Revelations will occur as frequently as we wish. The frequency of these occurrences will increase in direct proportion to the number of Truthful Light Forms we accept into our Consciousness and with Whatever Sound Waves We Allow to wash through our Awareness.

A simple truth of
LIFE…
(L)ight
(I)nspires
(F)ree
(E)nergy

LOVE…
(L)iving
(O)scillates
(V)aluable
(E)xperiences

Whenever we Become Aware of how all things work together for The Highest Purpose, we evolve our understanding. We Become more aware. We Become more Compassionate, kinder, and more Attentive. As we further develop these aspects, we simply Become more aware of Who and What we are. Upon Becoming more Fully Accepting of Who we are...Self Realization, we Begin Being What we are which is the Awareness of why we are here.

I AM AWARE.

8. THE SPIRIT'S FREE WILL

Do you see the dual meaning of the phrase *The Spirit's Free Will?*

Whichever your initial understanding of that phrase occurred to you is a key to better understanding yourself.

If what you understood *The Spirit's Free Will* to mean is that the Spirit is Free Will, then this signifies that you believe in Free Will being an aspect of your Consciousness. You are very Intuitive and Faithful that Everything will be fine. You are very creative as you associate aspects of your Being with concepts that explain our existence as Human Beings. You are more apt to ask *Why* questions such as *Why Are We Here?* You are comfortable with the process of Being as aware as you currently are.

If you understood this phrase to mean that the Spirit has Free Will, then you affix human qualities to processes that pertain to being human. You are very Logical and use Information to Become more knowledgeable. You use your knowledge to become more conscious. You are determined to know How things work and What is the purpose of things. You enjoy the process of Becoming more conscious.

Either way is beautiful and some are finding ways in which to take parallel paths. Some take the Red Pill while others take the Blue Pill. Some take both pills. Purple is my favorite color. All information is potentially useful. There are pieces of data embedded in every single experience that has ever occurred to every single living Being or Thing that has ever existed in The Universe.

What is Spirit? Spirit is our guide. Spirit is always useful. Spirit is always honest. Spirit will make you feel happy, nostalgic, grateful, and peaceful. Spirit will energize, and encourage you. Spirit is your FUEL

(F)reely
(U)nconditional
(E)xchange of
(L)ove

Many Beings refer to Spirits as The Spirit and consider it as part of A Sacred Triune, with God, The Father, The Son, and The Holy Ghost. We place human qualities on things to better understand them. Spirit has qualities, but being that they are not human, describing it as such is only maintaining a limited level of belief about them.

While we are trying to figure out the various aspects of a Thing, we also take possession of it. We claim to have Spirits. When we take ownership of anything, we form an attachment to it. When these attachments form, we will develop a desire to hold onto that thing. As with all attachments, an expectation forms as we believe that we deserve to continue to feel whatever that experience does in the creation of Emotions. Any assumptions regarding any of the processes of Life will only create degrees of suffering.

Spirits are not yours to keep or possess. Spirits are not ever going to harm you in any manner. One can have destructive intentions, but not Dark Spirits, as Spirits originate from The One. Spirits never deceive or destroy. Spirits are not permanently attached to Anything. Spirits are of The Spirit being felt by a Being.

Where is Spirit found? Since Spirit is invisible and gives off no Electro-magnetic Energy. Spirit is neither seen nor heard. Spirit is only felt. When we think that our Spirits are being lifted, that implies that our Spirit is supposed to be contained. We believe that we must guard our Spirits. Although this fear is reasonable, if we better understand what Spirit is, we can better understand how it functions and why we need it. Spirit is Everywhere and in Everything. Spirit is felt Wherever it is most useful.

We are wise to always pay attention to how we Feel. When we dismiss any of our Feelings or Emotions as not being useful, we are ignoring the messengers. We can be aware of our Spirit Level and can easily refill our Light Body Vessels by freely giving of Our Spirit at the earliest opportunity that presents itself. When we do our transferring of Energy then and there, we are showing Spirit The Way back into ourselves. Otherwise...we are placing an expectation of rewards by waiting until we have sufficient Energy to provide our service.

Interesting side note...Dark Forces are attracted to light bearers while Spirit, being invisible, can detect a lack of Light. Like attracts like. The Dark serves a very important purpose. The Dark Forces cause a path of destruction. This destruction, however, is the creation of a New Space, which is fresh and cleansed of all toxicity. The function of Evil becomes contrast. All of us have accused others of having Evil Spirits or believing that Dark Spirits can attack us. Be clear that their Spirit is of the Light, and even though it emits no radiation and is invisible, to describe Spirit in any manner such as Evil, Dark, Bad, or anything of the sort does nothing for you other than create division. The feeling of being other than Anything causes anxiety and frustration, and if gone unchecked, it will develop into hatred, fear, and terror.

When does Spirit present itself? Spirit is a free-roaming Entity that appears Whenever it is needed the most. The timing of the Spirit's Presence is always perfect. Spirit's Time always becomes apparent in The True Now. Even though Spirit is unseen, the Feeling is undeniable.

Who deserves to feel The Spirit? All Beings and Things deserve to Feel Spirit. Part of the reason for Anything to exist is to Feel The Spirit. Without the opportunity to Feel The Spirit, there is no reason to ever Be. Anyone willing to expand their Awareness will be inspired.

Spirit

inSPIRes

How does Spirit work? Spirit, being the Life Fuel, will always be presented when and where it is needed the most. Spirit can sense exactly the Splace in which it will be the most effective. Even though there is only the exact amount of Spirit that the Universe ever needs, there is always a sufficient amount available, as Spirit exists in direct proportion to the Physical Matter that concurrently exists in the Universe. Spirit resonates with the Void of Nothingness. When we are discouraged, disheartened, deceived, or on the verge of distraction, Spirit will always arrive on time, which is always the perfect time that we recognize as The Eternal Now.

As Human Beings, to Live, we are only required to do one thing that will allow for three minutes of Life. That one thing is to simply breathe. If we can maintain our means to provide Oxygen to our cells by not bleeding out, the secondary process that is required of us is to hydrate. H_2O maintains our Life Force for up to three days. Other nutrients and processes give us 30 days of Life.

Within these three time frames, we have sufficient time to serve whatever our purpose is. A majority of Human Beings are given between a few months to several years to fulfill their destiny. God provides us with Life, Consciousness, and Free Will. During however long of a duration of Time on Earth, we are granted, the one thing that is provided is Spirit. Without Spirit, we have no will to live. With infusions of Spirit, we find ourselves wherever we may be getting back up, dusting off ourselves, and forging ahead with newly Inspired Dreams and a Spirited Vision that always carries us into the future.

Whenever you feel low or in possession of Dense Energy. Lighten the load by using your Free Will to inspire others. Whenever you encourage or lift The Spirit of Another Being, no matter Who or What that Being is, and no matter how dense you felt going into that exchange, your Spirit Will Rise.

THIS IS THE WAY

9. THE SOUL IS GOD'S WILL

The Soul is the most misunderstood concept that has ever occurred to Human Beings. We have been led to believe that the Soul is yours. It is believed that you and every Human Being possess a Soul. This would make sense if it was true, but as with all things, one can decipher useful data from the transmission of any form of Energy. We can determine what is true based on how we feel about it.

We are led to believe that the Soul is yours to lose, sell, be possessed, or can even be sent to Hell. How do you feel about these concepts? Does this sound accurate or make any sense at all? Does it make you feel angry, anxious, and fearful? I have come to the Revelation that truth is recognized by how peacefully you feel upon its acceptance. The more profound the level of truth that is accepted, the equivalent levels of peacefulness are felt.

What is the Soul and what is its purpose? Let's examine some clues that will give us a better idea of what the Soul truly is.

The Tetragrammaton is YHVH. Many ancient languages are written to be read from right to left. So YHVH is below. Underneath the English letters is the Phoenician version and below that, the Hebrew version. What word jumps out immediately in the Phoenician version? HVHY.

God's name is said to be unpronounceable, but the letters do produce the sound /yah-way/ and are spelled, Yahweh. Some have spelled it Jehovah with a soft "j" pronouncing it as /yah-ho-vah/. Some have transformed it into another version of Adonai.

YHVH is derived from the phrase 'ehyehasherehyeh' translated to mean "I AM WHO I AM."

I have recognized that the most basic, pure, and accurate formation of God's name is not a word after all. It is a sound. That Sound is "AH" and is present in many versions of God's name. Both the word "god" and the name of the first letter in YHVH "yod" just so happen to possess the AH sound. Note the list of Gods, God-like Beings, and Messiahs with the AH sound. Below is a partial list.

Rah
Buddha
Krishna
Brahma
Shiva
Abraham
Yeshua
Jehovah
Allah
Muhammad

More clues as to what the Soul is can be seen in the connection between YHVH and the Four Fundamental Elements of Life Hydrogen, Oxygen, Nitrogen, and Carbon.

$Y(^7N)$

$H(^1H)$

$V(^8O)$

$H(^1H)$

First, take note that the most abundant element in the Universe is Hydrogen. It is perfectly synchronistic that the first letter of Hydrogen is called pronounced /eɪtʃ/ and spelled "aitch." Another sync is that it is the 8th letter in the English alphabet. Both the English (H) and the Hebrew (ה) possess the same /ay/ sound. In the word "Hydrogen," the (H) is pronounced /hah/ followed immediately with the /i/ just like you hear in "Eyes" as we see in the Phoenician version of YHVH.

Are any bells going off yet? Okay...let's proceed with reconnecting the dots. When you view the HVH, an archaic form of which is הוה (h-w-h), you can easily see the exact chemical makeup of the most valuable compound of the Universe Water.

$$^1H \quad ^1H$$
$$\searrow \nearrow$$
$$^8O$$

Your body is composed of 70-75% water as is the Earth. All living things sustain their life through all of the functions of water. Between H^2O and the prevalent abundance of Hydrogen, is there any question of God's existence? Even those who think that they do not believe in God, actually have a very profound understanding of one aspect of God, which is that of Nothingness.

As for what The Soul is...the answer is in the EYES. We have most likely heard the phrase *the eyes are the windows to the Soul.*

This is accurate and may I add that our Real Eyes have the same quality as a two-way mirror. When someone looks at our Eyes, they see a reflection of their Being. They see their reflection as well as figuratively see aspects of themselves in us.

The last clue regarding the Universe's Riddle as it pertains to the Soul is how a two-way mirror works and where it is used. Two-way mirrors are used in different circumstances, but all with the same intention. Two-way mirrors are used to view people from one room with those being observed only seeing their reflection.

Guess who views our Reality through our Eyes other than ourselves?

Yes...
GOD!
God lives through us, with us, because of us, and specifically for us. God remains in a constant state of change and is expanding in Awareness. God is going through the same process as we are.

HUMANS:

(3 STATES OF BEING)

1. MENTAL
2. PHYSICAL
3. EMOTIONAL

(4 ETERNAL ESSENCES)

1. CONSCIOUSNESS (WHO)
2. AWARENESS (WHAT)
3. SPIRIT (WAY)
4. SOUL (WHY)

GOD:

The Triune of Absolute Abilities of God are
as follows:

1. OMNISCIENCE
2. OMNIPRESENCE
3. OMNIPOTENCE
THE SOUL IS THE...

(S)PACE
(O)F
(U)NCONDITIONAL
(L)OVE

In this Space, God becomes more aware of what all Life Forms experience. As God Expands in Awareness, God becomes more knowing and remains Omniscient.

God is Everywhere Hydrogen is present, which is every Star and in every living organism. God's Presence is felt. God's Absolute Form cannot be seen by any, as it is the culmination of every bit of Energy in the

Universe. The physical aspect of God is seen in every Star and Every Living Organism. Another name for God is ELOHIM.

(E)VERY
(L)IVING
(O)RGANISM
(H)AS
(I)LLUMINATED
(M)ATTER

אֱלֹהִים

Elohim in Hebrew script with the letters going right-to-left: aleph-lamed-he-yud-mem. The first letter aleph is the first letter in the Hebrew alphabet. Remember the true sound of God, "AH," starts with the first letter in the English alphabet. God's History is Our Story. The chapters of Human History may be divided into Alpha-Beta chapters, but God's Story is Eternal and has no beginning or end. It does have a series of Alphas and Omegas. God's Power comes from the Omega. God's Divine Feminine Energy is Gaia. Through the Existence of Matter, the circle is complete. The word *"matter"* is derived from the Latin word "mater," which means mother. The words matrimony, matron, and matrix are derived from mater. Remember the phrase "ehyehasherehyeh" and its translation *I am who I am?*

What word is a title of respect for a Woman? MA'AM. God's wife was called ASHERAH.

I AM WHO I AM
0=OMEGA (Ω)
1=AH (Fah-There)
0=OHM(Mom, Home, Womb)
1=GOD
0=GAIA
1=LIGHT/DARK
0=SOUND/SILENCE
1=CONSCIOUSNESS
0=AWARENESS
1=YANG
0=YIN
1=ALPHA (α)

God's Power comes from all Life Forms and existing Energy. Since $E=mc^2$, and per The First Law of Thermodynamics, there is a continual recycling of all Energy. There is no finality. There is only transference of

Energy, which is only the transformation of information. The occurrence of New Life is reforming constantly.

The only question that remains is...*WHY?*

The Answer...

It's God's Will for All Beings to feel as Peaceful as God Currently Feels.

PEACEFUL NOW

I AM

10. ALL THAT MATTERS

All Beings Matter

All Things Matter

All Life Forms Matter

Knowledge is powerful, however, all that ever truly matters is the Present MOMent.

0=Yin

1=Yang

0=Omega

1=Alpha

0=Sound

1=Light

(God's Absolute Abilities)

OMNISCIENCE-Information

OMNIPRESENCE-Time

OMNIPOTENCE-Power

(3)MOM

(4)MOON

(5)MONTH

(6)MOMENT

(7)MONSOON

(8)MONUMENT

3+4+5+6+7+8=33

Omega=Ω/ω

33=$\omega\omega$

If you rely on what you think you know to believe in something, you limit your beliefs. If you use what you do know to either manipulate others or even destroy them, you may feel powerful as your Consciousness increases its rate of frequency, but you are not becoming more aware. You are remaining without knowing. That is ignorant. Whenever you are confused or frustrated, it is because you are not yet ready to better understand that concept, or Being.

Time is sensed and the effects of linear time are felt. When we lose track of time, we gain Peaceful Serenity by simply Being Sound. The MONumentalMOMents are stored as (M)e(M)ories. These memories are imprinted pieces of data that are stored in our DNA and passed down to our offspring.

God has many aspects, including Divine Feminine and Masculine Energies. The Masculine Alpha or "AH" sound is perfectly harMONius with the Feminine Omega "OHM" sound. Think of things in terms of electrical circuitry. Nikola Tesla proved that electricity has unlimited power when circuits are completed. He showed that circuits do not need to be dependent on cables of wire.

Unlimited Power is felt in the Present MOMent. Whenever we ignore how we feel, we are not paying attention to the only MOMent that matters, which is always NOW. When we are aware of how we feel in the True Now, we are completing the circuit of how we feel about what we know through our experiences. In other words, we are becoming more aware of what occurred to us as being useful information, no matter what happened to our experience.

Time in the linear sense is absolutely real. It is called Father Time, as the linear version is a very strict teacher. This is because Time causes friction. Without friction, we have no heat induction, energy transferences, chemical reactions, ionization, or any processes of Life. This is all an illusion but necessary to gain our attention. Whenever we do the only thing that is required with the learning process, which is paying attention to the MOMent, then and only then will Linear Time become irrelevant.

As per the First Law of Thermodynamics, which simply states that Energy is neither created nor destroyed, but merely transformed, we never actually waste Time or even lose Time. We are always learning whether or not we realize it or not. Data streams continue to be transmitted continuously from our first breath to the time of death, which is only another transfer of energy.

By simply paying attention, we are no longer Being in the Moment; we Become more aware of how we feel, which is Being Sound. By Being Sound, you do two things. You metaphorically become Sound in a Peaceful Sense and you become whatever Sound Wave Frequency you are harMOnizing with and simply Being. During these MOMents, Time becomes Infinite in nature. Infinite Time becomes most present in Eternal Space. The Feminine Energy aspects of Time and Space create

$$0 \times 0 \approx \infty$$

So what? Why does all of this information matter? Well...what we can do to become more aware is to refrain from overanalyzing everything. Instead of trying to know more, we can re-remember that The Way of Understanding is by Becoming more aware of simply Being Present. When you do this as a form of meditation, your True Power will be felt so strongly that you will be able to be in that Peaceful State whenever you wish. That Peaceful State of Being is powerful beyond measure. When something is beyond measure, it turns into an OMNI Aspect.

(OMN)IPRESENT
(OMN)IP(O)TENT

MOON Cycles occur MONthly for a reason. A WOMaN is presented with a painfully real process that incurs strong eMOtiONs. Men might be able to exert more physical force through their bodies; however, our tolerance for physical pain pales in comparison. Women are physically tougher than Men. Women are more gifted in MANifesting because they are better able at being present during those MOnuMentalMOMents like childbirth. Men simply would not be able to bear that burden.

Now...with that being said, with all due respect to Men, we endure a great deal of Mental trauma. Men are MENtally tough and able to disregard their EMotioNs to achieve what they set out to do. Men are skilled at using logic to solve problems.

Both Men and Women can be strong-willed in achieving what they strive to do. Both can balance their Yin/Yang Energies. Both can use their creative Imaginations. Both can be cOMpAssiONate, and hArMONiOus.

In the end, after all, is said and done, what can you gather from any experience? Have you honestly and thoroughly reviewed the information? Have you analyzed and assessed the data or did you prejudge and dismiss it by determining that it was not for you? Understanding everything never was necessary. Men like to figure things out but will only fool themselves if they think that they know what a Woman is thinking. When Men stop trying to solve a Woman's problems and just pay attention by listening, fewer conflicts will occur. When Women are allowed to express their feelings however they wish, more peacefulness will be felt by all.

Women will also be fooling themselves when they think that they understand how we feel. Men express their EMotioNs best when they are playing. It doesn't matter if they are playing video games, their guitar, or driving fast in their cars. If Men can freely express themselves in their way...more joy will be felt by all. We all realize how to express ourselves with our partners. That Sacred Union is a miracle as it not only creates new life but can sustain healing energies for both Beings. The circuit becomes complete through that reunion.

With family and friends, a simple hug is quite effective as well. When it is not time for a hug, a handshake or even a high-five goes a long way in lifting The Spirit.

Whatever you think the problem is, find a way to solve the issue with civil cOMMuNIcatION. Find the cONnectION. That ON switch will light up the room and inSPIRe the SPIRit to reappear. The solutION will become apPARENTly clear through active listening and sincerely honest conversatION.

NAMASTE

11. WHY DOES IT MATTER AT ALL?

What in the World is Dark Matter?
Why in the Hell Does it Exist?

Physicists seem hell-bent on finding a Dark Matter Particle. If you believe that E=mc² and Dark Matter gives off no radiation, then the first mistake is in the name. If the observable Universe (stars, planets, moons, comets, and asteroids) is only 5% of the matter, 95% of the Universe's mass is supposedly a combination of Dark Matter/Energy. If there is no detection of any Electromagnetic Radiation, then is it possible that Dark Matter is not *mattered* after all?

A few of these Physicists admit that they think they know what it is not, but have yet to determine what it is. They like to believe that they think outside of the box, but they remain attached to the idea that everything can be explained as being a particle.

They can see the effects that Gravity has on it through gravitational lensing, but cannot detect anything else that would indicate that it even exists at all.

I understand the desire to explain how things work. Whenever we get stuck or confused, we can utilize our intuitive mind as our logical mind has done everything possible to figure out the solution. Instead of trying to make a square peg fit into a round hole, why not allow for alternative ideas to flow?

Is it possible that gravitational lensing is occurring because of supermassive Black Holes?

Maybe we should be asking *why* questions to get us closer to the *how* and *what* questions.

WHY DOES DARK MATTER REALLY MATTER?

Science is the observation and study of measurement of the behavior of Energy in all known states of being. Physics is the study of the motion of particles and objects. Chemistry is the study of chemical reactions. Biology is the study of living organisms. Psychology is the study of our Mental State of Being. There are overlapping disciplines in these fields of study and these connections explain how everything is related. All are one and everything is exactly as it is supposed to be.

With all of the technology that we have to observe, analyze, and record data, scientists are stuck on the notion that there must be a Dark Matter Particle. If a DMP can exist, then it may be discovered. After all...*ANYTHING IS POSSIBLE.*

Words do matter, however, as they define that which can be defined. Anything can be defined, including that which is immeasurable. A definition does not describe everything about anything that is being assessed or analyzed. We can define Space as being the 3rd Dimension, but we are describing a form that possesses three dimensions (length, width, and height). Space is immeasurable. Space is a thing, but it possesses the aspect of nothingness that cannot be measured. We can define Time for example as being the interval between two occurrences. We can also use subdivisions to create a way to measure linear Time, but can not measure Time in its absolute state of being as it is immeasurable as it is infinite. The same applies to Gravity. We have defined it as one of the forces of nature when it is a field of varying degrees of density. The relation between mass and Gravity can be observed, as Gravity affects the motion (spin) of objects, as well as their movement about other objects (rotation), and their position in the Universe, which is where it travels in Space.

All three concepts—Space, Time, and Gravity—matter because they affect Matter. Neither Space, Time, or Gravity can be observed in its absolute state of being. We are only able to see how these three properties of the Universe interact with each other and how they are utilized to transform Electro-magnetic Energy into the various states of Matter.

WHAT IS MATTER?

According to Einstein, $E=mc^2$. The matter is Energy in a state of being existent. We call this state of being Reality. Scientists use the term

Physicality. This is why physics is the study of Matter. The analysis of how matter behaves is formed, and how it changes over Time is how we have come to know what we do about observable particles.

If Dark Matter emits no Electromagnetic Radiation whatsoever, then it cannot be observed. All observable EM Radiation has already been classified, so to call Dark Matter by a paradoxical name is the cause for the confusion. Even though the debate between the certainty of Einstein's theories conflicts with the uncertainty of Quantum Physics continues, the premise of $E=mc^2$ seems resolute. Until someone can refute the connection between Energy and Matter, we can use $E=mc^2$ as a defining tool to describe what exists in our Physical Reality. The word "Dark" implies that the thing is invisible. If we believe in the foundation that $E=mc^2$, can we agree that searching for an invisible object will never yield the desired result and therefore, a Dark Matter Particle will never be found because, by its definition, is simply unobservable?

This lack of "measurable" proof does not determine our ability to better understand that which is named *Dark Matter*. All that we have to do to better understand anything is to accept that some of the information about that which is being studied will not be observable data.

So what type of information is unobservable but still useful? I believe that the most useful information is felt. Through our feelings, we are enabled to become more aware of what is occurring and therefore more fully understood. Our logical mind processes information that is observed through our physical brain. The acceptance of Light Forms brings Illumination. All Illumination causes our Consciousness to increase its rate of frequency. This is referred to as Enlightenment.

Our intuitive mind processes Sound Forms that are felt through our Heart Space. The allowance of Sound Frequencies brings feelings of Peacefulness. All Peacefulness results in the expansion of our Awareness. This Awareness is indescribable but is a Spiritual experience.

WHAT IS SPIRIT?

Spirit is our Life Force. SPIRit is the fuel that inSPIRes us. Spirit lifts our bodies. The SpIRIt causes the RISIng of the rate of conscious frequency to increase. Spirit allows us to feel all of our Senses including our Sense of Space (Proprioception), our Sense of Motion through the effects of Gravity, and our Sense of Time. Spirit allows us to feel emotions, physical pain, and pleasure, as well as mental satisfaction. Spirit is immeasurable as it can only be felt. The effects of Spirit can be observed, but Spirit itself is invisible. Those effects are experienced through our Physical Bodies. Those bodies including Living Organisms and Other Beings are particles of matter that are classified as Things.

The Absolute Duality of the Universe seems to be that of Physicality and Spirituality.

Physicality includes anything observable through our naked eyes or tools of technology. Everything in the known Universe that falls under $E=mc^2$. Spirituality is the aspect of all other things that exist. The list that is of the Spirit includes, thought forms, feelings, and concepts such as Love or God.

SO...WHAT IS DARK MATTER?

The answer to this question has become evident through the processing of pertinent information. I propose that Dark Matter is Pure Spirit. Everything that exists becomes a Reality because of Spirit. That which cannot be observed, but only felt, becomes real through Spirit.

Everything in the known Universe that comes into our Reality is born of The Spirit. Everything of a Physical nature comes from Nothing of a Spiritual nature. Spiritual Actuality becomes the cause of Physical Reality, being the effect that further causes the transformation of Consciousness back into The Absolute Stillness and Perfect Silence of Pure Awareness. I contend that there is a pure duality that is occurring in our known Universe.

0=Spirit
1=Energy
0=Actuality
1=Reality
0=Awareness
1=Consciousness

I FEEL QUIETLY PEACEFUL
IN MY INNERSTANDING OF
WHAT I BELIEVE SPIRIT
TO HAVE ALWAYS BEEN,
HOW IT IS CURRENTLY BEING,
AND WILL ETERNALLY BE.

ABOUT THE AUTHOR

 Michael W. Evrard was born in El Monte, California on 1/20/1970, and was adopted with his twin brother Patrick soon after their birth by Jesse and Wilma Evrard. He was raised in Glendora, California, not far from Los Angeles. Today, Michael is a musician, artist, and philosopher living in Southern California, whose spiritual journey began one fateful day in 1973.

The approach he takes with his research and writing is straightforward. He finds the connections between science, spirituality, religion, psychology, philosophy, and faith, and provides subjective and empirical evidence to prove that feelings are the most effective form of communication in the Universe and the most effective language due to its ease of translation.

He is very passionate about his beliefs and views *feelings* as being the language of God. He completed the Sight/Sound/Spirit trilogy on 8/8/2021 and is offering this series as an introduction to his life's work. He is honored to have the opportunity to share what he believes, and he loves speaking about any topics that pertain to consciousness. Being that all things in the universe are sentient, he enjoys talking about literally anything.

Connect with Michael in the public "SIGHT/SOUND/SPIRIT" Facebook group and the "Michael W. Evrard" author page.

Also from Stone Compass Press

Why Are We Here on Earth?
*(Book I of the Sight/Sound/Spirit Trilogy,
by Michael W. Evrard, 2022)*

$16.95

Anti-Aging Encyclopedia of Natural Health (Fourth Edition)
(by Joseph Marion, 2021)

$79.00

Black Robe: The Kempo/Kajukenbo Connection
(by David Tavares, 2017)

$25.00

Hawai'i Vortex Field Guide
(by Zach Royer, 2014)

$14.95

Pyramid Rising: Planetary Acupuncture to Combat Climate Change
(by Zach Royer, 2012)

$14.95

Stone Compass Press specializes in paperback, hardback, and eBook publishing with a focus on Metaphysical, Esoteric, Paranormal, Science Fiction, and Educational genres. Take your first steps to a successful writing career at www.StoneCompassPress.com.

We offer some of the highest royalties in the USA!
$0 upfront costs* (*complete ebook manuscripts)

Phone: (808) 238-2264
Email: info@zoat.org
Web: http://www.stonecompasspress.com

Sponsor your business with Hawaii's fastest growing publishing & media company!

Stone Compass Press
2023 Sponsorship Rate

Size: 4.5" x 7.5", 5.5" x 8.5" or 6.5" x 9.5" (w x h)

~~$250~~
$200

*Price displayed is for our 3-month quarterly rate.

Learn more or purchase a sponsorship at

www.StoneCompassPress.com/advertising

HAWAI'I VORTEX TOURS, RETREATS & OTHER ACTIVITIES SPECIFICALLY DESIGNED TO ENHANCE YOUR EXPERIENCE IN PARADISE.

TUNE IN TO THE VORTEX. CHARGE WITH THE ʻĀINA. TRANSFORM WITH ALOHA.

www.HawaiiVortex.com

Web design, small business optimization & more at www.ZOAT.org.

www.ingramcontent.com/pod-product-compliance
Lightning Source LLC
Chambersburg PA
CBHW051525150726

47997CB00001B/394